Amazing Disciples

Powerful Keys for Personal Evangelism

A 13-Week Lesson Book Presented
by the Amazing Facts Center of Evangelism (AFCOE)

Amazing Disciples

Powerful Keys for Personal Evangelism
A 13-Week Lesson Book Presented
by the Amazing Facts Center of Evangelism (AFCOE)

Amazing Disciples
Powerful Keys for Personal Evangelism

Copyright © 2017 by Amazing Facts, Inc.

Published by Amazing Facts, Inc.
P.O. Box 1058
Roseville CA 95678
916-434-3880
www.afbookstore.com

Written by Carissa McSherry
Cover by Daniel Hudgens
Layout by Greg Solie ▪ Altamont Graphics

ISBN 978-1-58019-653-6

Table of Contents

Everyone is on a journey of faith. Let's consider the most effective ways of responding to objections, while lifting up Jesus and reaching the heart.

How do you lead others to make a decision for Jesus? This week's aim is to take the fear out of asking for decisions, using the "four Cs of gaining decisions."

We will consider how to lead someone to a saving relationship with Jesus Christ and give a sound answer to the question, "What must I do to be saved?"

While the church should proclaim the gospel, it should also establish new believers and make them disciples.

Learn why former members have left the church and very practical principles for bringing them back into the fold.

Foreword

Christians are, by definition, followers of Christ. And the reason we follow Him is because of love—for God and for our neighbor. Further, if we love the Lord with all of our hearts and souls, what is supremely important to Him will be a priority to us.

So we must ask, What really matters to God?

They say you can tell where people's priorities are by the way they spend their time and money. "Where your treasure is, there your heart will be also" (Matthew 6:21). We can quickly understand, then, the priorities of God by the price He paid to redeem people. The Father so loves the world that He gave His beloved Son; and the Son so loves perishing humanity that He willingly came to earth for thirty-three years to suffer and sacrifice His life to redeem it.

Jesus summarized His mission with these words: "The Son of Man has come to seek and to save that which was lost" (Luke 19:10). There you have it. God has mobilized all of heaven's resources—His Spirit, His creative power, His angels, and His Son, who paid an enormous price to rescue those who are willing to be saved. And as His followers, His priorities should be our priorities.

This is the overarching message of this exciting *Amazing Disciples* study lesson book. It's all about learning how to better live the life of a disciple and better do the work of winning souls to His eternal kingdom. This is the work that matters most to God.

Amazing Disciples can be used for personal devotions and Bible study groups, but it's also perfectly designed for a church that wants to explore how every member can become more effective at outreach. It's both inspiring and practical—and I believe it will make a tremendous difference in your church family.

And finally, a special thanks to Carissa McSherry, who has beautifully coalesced fifty years of Amazing Facts evangelism training into a simple yet power-packed study series that will enrich all who use it.

—Doug Batchelor
President, Amazing Facts

In developing and writing this lesson book, I am indebted to each of the AFCOE directors and personal evangelism teachers who have served since the school was established in 2001. Much of their course content, which appears in our AFCOE syllabus and other course materials, has been used throughout this guide or has otherwise heavily inspired these lessons. I'd also like to thank Pastor Jëan Ross, evangelism director at Amazing Facts, whose *Empowered Church* manual is used extensively in section two. Finally, a special thank-you to Chuck Holtry, AFCOE director, for his encouragement, insight, and guidance during this project. With these vital contributions, the constant guidance of God's Word, and the careful influence of Ellen G. White, the team at AFCOE hopes and prays these lessons will help you become a better, more inspired soul winner.

—Carissa McSherry
AFCOE Assistant Director

Week One
Divine Commission

FOCUS
"Go therefore and make disciples of all the nations, baptizing them in the name of the Father and of the Son and of the Holy Spirit, teaching them to observe all things that I have commanded you; and lo, I am with you always, even to the end of the age" (Matthew 28:19, 20).

INTRODUCTION
Though given nearly 2,000 years ago to a motley group of disciples, our mission as Christians today remains the same: "Go and make disciples." Unless we clearly understand and internalize the marching orders of our Master, we can never fulfill this mission.

What is God's calling for my life?
What is my role in evangelism?
How can I help hasten the coming of Christ?

If you've ever asked yourself these questions—you'll enjoy our first lesson, which provides biblical, clear, practical answers—and more—all while thrilling your heart with our heavenly Father's beautiful calling for His people today!

David Livingstone once said, "If a commission by an earthly king is considered an honor, how can a commission by a Heavenly King be considered a sacrifice?" Truly! No supposed sacrifice—a prosperous career, a promising relationship, or a life of ease—can be compared with the infinite sacrifice of Jesus Christ! That's why there is no greater calling, and no higher privilege, than to be His ambassador.

THIS WEEK IN THE SCRIPTURES
Prayerfully read these passages before beginning this week's study.

- Matthew 28:18–20
- Luke 19:1–10
- Acts 4:32–35
- Mark 5:1–20

The Last Message

Read — Matthew 24:14 and the following from *Christ's Object Lessons*, p. 69:

Christ is waiting with longing desire for the manifestation of Himself in His church. When the character of Christ shall be perfectly reproduced in His people, then He will come to claim them as His own.

React — In these passages, what two reasons are given for why Christ has not yet come? Are these passages conflicting or harmonious? Explain.

_____

_____

_____

Has anyone ever defamed your character? Whether someone at work purposely backstabbed you with a white lie or a trusted friend spread unfair gossip about you—it hurt!

But now recall the pain when a family member inquired, "Is it really true?"

To be doubted, to be misunderstood, is one of the most painful experiences we can encounter. Well, the heart of God knows this feeling all too well—on an unfathomable, universal scale. Not only does it hurt Him, it hurts His creation.

Our Father longs to reveal His true character to the world!

Matthew 24:14 reminds us that we must be witnesses of the gospel that we preach. In other words, it must be our *experience*, not a mere theoretical knowledge or a family testimony from the past carried on through the generations. We must be living witnesses of what we personally have "seen" and "heard" (1 John 1:1–3).

Regardless of how many Bible tracts a person might receive or sermons he might hear, the good news is not fully preached unless God's character is being revealed through the daily lives of His people! "When He comes, in that Day, to be glorified in His saints and to be admired among all those who believe, because our testimony among you was believed" (2 Thessalonians 1:10).

Read — Luke 19:1–10

React — Beyond his finances, what did Zacchaeus give up in his search for a relationship with Christ? In what ways did Zacchaeus' conversion alter his life? What lessons can we personally learn and apply from this story?

_____

_____

_____

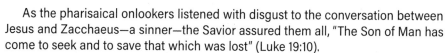

As the pharisaical onlookers listened with disgust to the conversation between Jesus and Zacchaeus—a sinner—the Savior assured them all, "The Son of Man has come to seek and to save that which was lost" (Luke 19:10).

The glories of heaven and the beauty of His Father's presence were no longer enough to satisfy the heart of Christ. His children were hurting, their understanding of Him tragically warped. He willingly forfeited the perfection of heaven to enter and save a broken world.

Eddy Ho, a foreign missionary, put it this way: "God was the first ever missionary when in Genesis 3:8 He went out in search of two sinners who had rebelled against Him in order to bring them back into fellowship with Him."

Discuss — Christ still carries the burden for souls on His heart! But the question is, Does this burden also weigh on your heart—and on the hearts of all His people? Why or why not?

_____

_____

_____

Lingering on the Shore

Read — Matthew 28:18–20 and 1 Corinthians 3:8, 9

React — Under whose authority do we evangelize? With whom must we continually labor?

_____

_____

_____

The parting words of a loved one are not soon forgotten. The words spoken just before the last breath are indelibly ingrained upon sorrowful, broken hearts.

Jesus knew that His departure was near.

He looked out on a group of feeble believers, weakly led by eleven bickering men who were _still_ seeking supremacy in the kingdom of God. Remarkably, Jesus did not question their unbelief; He did not rebuke their divisive ways. Rather, Jesus looked upon these dysfunctional believers and gave them a mission—a mission that still unites His children today! "Go therefore and make disciples."

Though Christ would soon depart, He left believers with the promise that they would never labor alone. We are God's fellow workers, even until "the end of the age." There is no higher calling, no greater purpose, than to be a co-laborer with Jesus Christ!

Read — 1 John 4:11 and 1 John 3:16–18

React — If we love Christ, what will we be motivated to do?

_____

_____

_____

David Livingstone wisely remarked, "Sympathy is no substitute for action." Love for Christ does not simply produce sympathy—it motivates us to action. "The heart that rests most fully upon Christ will be most earnest and active in labor for Him" (_Steps to Christ_, p. 71).

Reflect — "In the contemplation of Christ we linger on the shore of a love that is measureless. We endeavor to tell of this love, and language fails us. We consider His life on earth, His sacrifice for us, His work in heaven as our advocate, and the mansions He is preparing for those who love Him, and we can only exclaim, O the height and depth of the love of Christ! 'Herein is love, not that we loved God, but that He loved us, and sent His Son to be the propitiation for our sins.' 'Behold, what manner of love the Father hath bestowed upon us, that we should be called the sons of God.' 1 John 4:10; 3:1. In every true disciple this love, like sacred fire, burns on the altar of the heart" (_The Acts of the Apostles_, pp. 333, 334).

Discuss — What can we do to keep this sacred fire burning in our hearts?

_____

_____

_____

Finding Unity

Read — Acts 4:32 and John 17:20, 21

React — What is the greatest sign of a converted church? What is the greatest demonstration of the reality of God?

_____

_____

_____

It has been estimated that there are more than 30,000 distinct Protestant denominations in the world. The devil delights in this pervasive division!

Yet the heart of Christ yearns to reveal a people fully united in Him, just as in His early church.

Ellen White beautifully penned, "We are exhorted to love as brethren, to be kind, courteous, forbearing, in honor preferring one another. Love for God and for one another constitutes the divine credentials which the children of God bear to the world. 'By this,' said Jesus, 'shall all men know that ye are my disciples, if ye have love one to another'" (*Historical Sketches of the Foreign Missions of the Seventh-day Adventists*, p. 214).

Please note that unity is never based on conformity; unity can be found only in the presence of Jesus Christ! (John 12:32). True believers will worship Him in both "Spirit and truth" (John 4:23, 24).

Read — "Wherever a church is established, all the members should engage actively in missionary work. They should visit every family in the neighborhood, and know their spiritual condition" (*Christian Service*, p. 12).

React — What percentage of church members should be actively engaged in evangelism? Why is it that so many Christians seem hesitant to share their faith? (See also Romans 1:16.)

_____

_____

_____

Do you know someone who has "fallen head over heels in love"?

It is difficult for him to have a conversation about anything other than the object of his affections. You *never* have to remind him to talk about his loved one, because it seems as though he can speak of nothing else!

Well, what if our experience with Christ were the same? What if evangelism were not something we "do" but the very joy and natural expression of our heart?

Like the apostles of old, we could truly say with joy in our hearts, "Chain me up. Throw me in prison. But I can do nothing less than speak of the One whom I love!" (See Acts 5:27–29, 40–42.)

Discuss — How can we develop a love for Christ as great as the disciples had? What is the basis of every healthy relationship? How does this relationship essential apply to our relationship with Christ?

_____

_____

_____

Saved to Serve

Read — Mark 5:1–20

React — How did Jesus' reaction differ from that of the apostles? After experiencing the healing of divine grace, what did the demoniac desire to do?

_____

_____

_____

The shrieks of demons pierced the air, sending shivers down the spine of the fleeing disciples. Suddenly, the risk of facing a stormy sea seemed far more appealing than an encounter with a naked and filthy demon-possessed man, whose blood flowed freely from self-inflicted wounds.

Yet Jesus knew no fear.

In the presence of Christ, the demons fled and sanity was restored.

After experiencing such a miraculous, healing touch, the former demoniac longed to remain in the presence of Christ! But God had a different calling for him: "Go home to your friends, and tell them what great things the Lord has done for you, and how He has had compassion on you" (Mark 5:19).

Yes—in the face of a former demoniac, who was screaming and cursing the Savior only minutes before, Christ saw a missionary.

Read — Acts 22:15 and 1 John 1:1–4

React — What should we share with others? Why is our personal experience the most powerful witness that can be given?

_____

_____

_____

Why does God use weak, erring human beings to spread the gospel to the world? After all, He is not limited. He once used a rooster to bring conviction to a sinful man. He spoke through a donkey to humble a prophet. Even stones can cry out! So why then does God use *us*?

Ellen White reminded us, "God could have reached His object in saving sinners without our aid; but in order for us to develop a character like Christ's, we must share in His work. In order to enter into His joy—the joy of seeing souls redeemed by His sacrifice—we must participate in His labors for their redemption" (*The Desire of Ages*, p. 142).

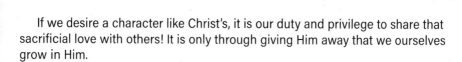

If we desire a character like Christ's, it is our duty and privilege to share that sacrificial love with others! It is only through giving Him away that we ourselves grow in Him.

Discuss — In what ways does soul winning bring us closer to Jesus?

_____

_____

_____

Tools You Can Use!

A cool breeze rustled the garden trees. With one last glance behind him and a racing heart, Nicodemus gazed upon the moonlit form of the Man he sought.

"Rabbi," he began, "we know that You are a teacher come from God" (John 3:2). Thus commenced a conversation that has been retold through the generations. Why? Because it records a beautiful promise of a God of love that we still claim today! (See verse 16.)

Nicodemus was a religious leader, highly acclaimed among his peers. Yet his heart searched for something more. Soon his questions found their answer in the presence of Jesus. But even still, it would be another three years before Nicodemus would give his life to Jesus Christ.

Even the most powerful soul winner who ever lived—Jesus—did not always see immediate results. And sometimes, seekers even walked away. (See Luke 18:18–23.)

But Jesus never gave up!

We can get discouraged when it appears that our evangelism efforts fail. We may even question our calling. But we must never forget the experience of Christ. "Let us not grow weary while doing good, for in due season we shall reap if we do not lose heart" (Galatians 6:9).

Apply — Here are three tips for being a powerful soul-winner for Jesus Christ!

1. Be prayerful.

Hudson Taylor, a fearless Christian who was foremost in establishing missionaries in China, said: "God uses men who are weak and feeble enough to lean on Him." Do we recognize our need of constant dependence upon Him? "At the sound of fervent prayer, Satan's whole host trembles" (*Counsels for the Church*, p. 319).

2. Be persistent.

Charles Spurgeon humorously stated: "By perseverance the snail reached the ark." How true this concept is in evangelism! Never, ever give up. Claim Galatians 6:9 and keep moving forward in faith!

3. Be personable.

"Those who have been most successful in soul-winning were men and women who did not pride themselves on their ability, but who in humility and faith sought to help those about them. Jesus did this very work. He came close to those whom He desired to reach" (*Gospel Workers*, p. 194).

Words to Live By

Every church should be a training school for Christian workers. Its members should be taught how to give Bible readings, how to conduct and teach Sabbath school classes, how best to help the poor and to care for the sick, how to work for the unconverted (*Lift Him Up*, p. 311).

If God calls you to be a missionary, don't stoop to be a king (Jordan Grooms).

The best remedy for a sick church is to put it on a missionary diet (David Livingstone).

We are to be consecrated channels, through which the heavenly life is to flow to others. The Holy Spirit is to animate and pervade the whole church, purifying and cementing hearts. Those who have been buried with Christ in baptism are to rise to newness of life. ... Upon us is laid a sacred charge. The commission has been given us: "Go therefore and make disciples of all nations" (Matthew 28:19 RSV). ... You are dedicated to the work of making known the gospel of salvation (*Testimonies for the Church*, Vol. 9, p. 20).

Weekly Challenge! Who is in your circle of influence? Is God calling you to reach friends or family members? This week, pray and ask God to reveal people you can reach for His kingdom! Write down five names and share them with your outreach or prayer partner for prayer and increased accountability.

"Here Come the Christians," Part One

As our car stopped in front of the apartment complex, we noted the police officer making his daily round through the neighborhood. With prayer and a deep breath, we confidently stepped out of the car and walked toward the concrete stairs.

The sickening-sweet smell of marijuana engulfed us as we dared to approach the dilapidated buildings. All eyes quickly turned to stare at us—the intruders—but we just returned their gawks with warm smiles.

"Oh, look. Here come the Christian girls," a man flippantly remarked, laughing with his friends. With a polite smile, we hurried our way up to her apartment while the men turned their attention back to another hit from their marijuana joints.

As young AFCOE students, nothing could deter us from reaching this community for Christ!

Betsy quickly opened the door and flashed a bright smile. "I've been looking forward to this all day long!" her raspy voice declared.

Her life had never been one of ease. Abandonment, abuse, drugs, and homelessness had all left their marks upon her at one time or another.

As we eased into her well-worn, overstuffed couch, we excitedly turned to that day's lesson: "The Coming King." How eagerly she hung onto every word as a picture was painted of a God of love who soon will come back to take her to her forever home.

After several weeks of studying with Betsy, an Amazing Facts prophecy series came to town. Each night Betsy would attend with a Bible in her hand and a nearly toothless grin spread across her face. She sat on the edge of her seat, amazed at the truth she was learning! Betsy eagerly awaited the day when she could become a member of that small Sabbath-keeping church.

But little did she know the life-threatening attack the devil would soon unleash upon her.

Continued next week ...

19

Week Two
Christ's Method Alone

FOCUS

"If you extend your soul to
the hungry and satisfy the
afflicted soul, then your light
shall dawn in the darkness,
and your darkness shall be
as the noonday. The LORD will
guide you continually, and
satisfy your soul in drought"
(Isaiah 58:10, 11).

INTRODUCTION

No matter how imaginative we may be with outreach ideas, Christ's way of
evangelism should always be our primary model.

"Christ's method alone will give true success in reaching the people. The
Savior mingled with men as one who desired their good. He showed His sympathy
for them, ministered to their needs, and won their confidence. Then He bade
them, 'Follow Me'" (*The Ministry of Healing*, p. 143). Notice Christ's method for
reaching hearts:

1. Mingled with people

2. Desired their good

3. Showed sympathy for their problems

4. Ministered to their needs

5. Thus won their confidence

6. *Then* called them to follow Him

We've learned that Christ's method alone will bring *true* success. Does that
mean there could be "false success"? Or even "apparent success"?

Jonathan Edwards was a famous revivalist during the mid-eighteenth century.
His most widely known sermon, "Sinners in the Hands of an Angry God," left a
lasting impact on countless souls.

While the church was gathered in hushed silence, Edwards preached, "The God
that holds you over the Pit of Hell, much as one holds a Spider, or some loathsome
Insect, over the Fire, abhors you, and is dreadfully provoked; his Wrath towards

you burns like Fire; he looks upon you as worthy of nothing else, but to be cast into the Fire."

His chilling description was concluded with the appeal, "Therefore, let everyone that is out of Christ, now awake and fly from the Wrath to come." With moans of grief and tears of repentance, naturally the many gathered made the desired decision. But did it last?

Romans 2:4 states that "the goodness of God leads you to repentance." The effects of fear—or the ecstasy of entertainment—will not bring true success. Genuine success is found only in a personal relationship with Christ as we apply His true method in reaching souls today!

THIS WEEK IN THE SCRIPTURES

Prayerfully read these passages before beginning this week's study.

- Matthew 9:1–8; 18–22
- John 5:1–9
- Isaiah 58
- 1 Kings 17:8–16
- Acts 8:26–39

Seeing with His Eyes

Read — Matthew 9:1-8

React — Which did Christ offer first: healing or forgiveness? Why did He choose this order?

_____

_____

_____

The scribes leaned forward in eager anticipation. What was Jesus going to do with that paralytic—the man who, in their eyes, was obviously a wretched sinner?

Though not a word of his desire for healing is recorded in the biblical account, the desire of the disabled man seemed evident to all. Yet Jesus, bypassing the physical ailment, looked with compassion into the heart of the guilt-ridden and said, "Son, be of good cheer; your sins are forgiven you."

Be of good cheer? But he was still paralyzed! How could he rejoice? *The Ministry of Healing* explains:

Hope takes the place of despair, and joy of oppressive gloom. The man's physical pain is gone, and his whole being is transformed. Making no further request, he lay in peaceful silence, too happy for words. ... The paralytic found in Christ healing for both the soul and the body. He needed health of soul before he could appreciate health of body. Before the physical malady could be healed, Christ must bring relief to the mind, and cleanse the soul from sin. This lesson should not be overlooked. There are today thousands suffering from physical disease who, like the paralytic, are longing for the message, "Thy sins are forgiven." The burden of sin, with its unrest and unsatisfied desires, is the foundation of their maladies. They can find no relief until they come to the Healer of the soul. The peace which He alone can impart would restore vigor to the mind and health to the body (pp. 76, 77).

Discuss — What lessons can we apply from this example? How can we learn to truly see with the eyes of Christ? Refer to 1 Samuel 16:7 and James 1:5.

_____

_____

_____

Nurturing Faith

Read — Matthew 9:18–22

React — How did Jesus demonstrate His approval of this woman and her act of faith?

_____

_____

_____

Time was of the essence.

Every moment that passed was excruciating to the father of a dying twelve-year-old girl. But the pressure of the crowd and the pleas of a desperate father were not enough to distract Christ from the need at hand.

A woman. Depressed, discouraged, penniless, and lonely after twelve long years of illness. According to *The Ministry of Healing* ...

Christ knew every thought of her mind, and He was making His way to where she stood. He realized her great need, and He was helping her to exercise faith (p. 60).

Similarly, when we seek after God in prayer, we can know with certainty that Christ is already moving toward us, helping us to exercise and grow in our faith.

Read — John 5:1-9

React — What question did Christ ask of the infirmed man? Why was this question important, seeing that the answer seemed obvious?

_____

_____

_____

"Do you want to be made well?" a kind voice inquired. The hope these words inspired in his heart was quickly beaten back as the invalid recounted the impossibilities of his situation. But Jesus, seeing that glimpse of faith, looked beyond the excuses and empowered this infirmed man to rise and walk.

You see, Christ never forces the will of others. He desires that we "may prosper in all things and be in health" (3 John 1:2), but the choice remains ours alone. Though He stands and knocks patiently, it is our decision whether or not to open the door (Revelation 3:20; Joshua 24:15).

Healed through Service

Read — Proverbs 3:7 and Isaiah 58:6–11

React — What will satisfy our souls? According to this passage, what is the result of living a Christ-centered and others-focused life?

_____

_____

_____

When we take our eyes off of ourselves and place them on others, lives are truly transformed—both theirs and ours!

During a 2002 study reported in _Pain Management Nursing_, it was discovered that "nurses suffering from chronic pain experienced declines in their pain intensity and decreased levels of disability and depression when they began to serve as peer volunteers for others also suffering from chronic pain. 'Despite encountering challenges, the rewards of this altruistic endeavor outweighed any frustrations experienced by volunteers with chronic pain.' "[1]

According to an article in _Psychology Today_, "volunteering is associated with lower depression, increased well-being, and a 22 percent reduction" in the risk of an early death.[2]

These findings confirm the writings of Ellen White. "You who are suffering with poor health, there is a remedy for you. If thou clothe the naked, and bring the poor that are cast out to thy house, and deal thy bread to the hungry, 'then shall thy light break forth as the morning, and thine health shall spring forth speedily.' Doing good is an excellent remedy for disease" (_Testimonies for the Church_, Vol. 2, p. 29).

Read — 1 Kings 17:8–16

React — What must this woman do before she could be assured of provision from God? Was this an easy decision?

_____

_____

_____

With a heavy heart, she began to prepare what would be their very last meal. How could she explain her grief and inability to provide, to her hungry child?

---

1   http://psychcentral.com/blog/archives/2015/10/19/helping-someone-else-can-alleviate-depression

2   https://www.psychologytoday.com/blog/the-empathy-gap/201308/the-caring-cure-can-helping-others-help-yourself

Her troubled thoughts were interrupted by the words of a stranger requesting nourishment. In an act of incredible faith, she denied herself and her child what appeared to be their last morsel of food in order to provide for the needs of a prophet, trusting in his promise of continued provision. Her faith was rewarded and his promise was indeed fulfilled!

Discuss — How does this principle relate to us in ministry? What resources or blessings do we have that we might be tempted to hoard? How can we more fully surrender these to Christ and use them to minister to our communities?

_____

_____

_____

Divine Appointments

Read — John 1:40–42 and John 4:27–30

React — How did these individuals respond after hearing the good news of salvation?

_____

_____

_____

Upon hearing the good news, Andrew raced to his brother Peter. "We have found the Messiah," Andrew exclaimed as he then brought Peter to Jesus. Later, when times seemed desperate and food was scarce, Andrew brought a little boy with five loaves and two small fish to Jesus (John 6:5–13). And toward the close of Christ's earthly ministry, devout Greek worshippers implored His disciple Philip, "Sir, we wish to see Jesus." Philip and Andrew were ambassadors for Christ (John 12:20–22).

You see, Andrew was never known for being an eloquent speaker. He did not stand out as a commanding leader among the apostles. But Andrew certainly knew how to be an ambassador for Christ!

Read — Acts 8:26–39

React — Where did the angel tell Philip to go? From our limited vantage point, does it sound wise to remove a successful evangelist from numerous souls in the city and send him to a wilderness?

_____

_____

_____

The request may have sounded illogical, but Philip did not hesitate to arise and go. He was soon led by the Spirit to the chariot of an Ethiopian eunuch, a man of great authority. This incredible divine appointment led to the conversion and baptism of this sincere seeker of truth, and ultimately, to the gospel spreading throughout Ethiopia!

Discuss — Does God have divine appointments for us today? How can we ensure we don't miss these golden witnessing opportunities?

_____

_____

_____

Tools You Can Use!

Jesus knew how to effectively meet the needs of people. He was always interested in those around Him. He looked to see what they were seeking, what their longings were, what their needs were.

Those who have been most successful in soul-winning were men and women who did not pride themselves on their ability, but who in humility and faith sought to help those about them. Jesus did this very work. He came close to those whom He desired to reach (*Gospel Workers*, p. 194).

This is demonstrated most tangibly through the Gospel of John:

In John 2, Jesus met a social need. After running out of wine at a wedding feast, Jesus' mother pled with Him to provide for their social need. In response, Jesus turned six stone jars of water into refreshing new wine, thus alleviating the host's social embarrassment and providing a spiritual lesson.

In John 3, Jesus met a spiritual need. In the midst of the garden, under the cover of night, a Pharisee met with Jesus. This secret discussion eventually led to Nicodemus accepting Christ as his personal Savior. Jesus looked beyond Nicodemus' religious façade and met his spiritual need.

In John 4, Jesus met an emotional need. Viewed as untouchable by the Jews and an outcast by those of her own country, her heart craved healing and true love. Though she had five husbands previously and was currently living with another man, the yearnings of her heart weren't satisfied until she met Jesus, who offered her emotional support by treating her with respect and by demonstrating the tremendous value God placed on her.

In John 5, Jesus met a physical need. "Do you want to be made whole?" He asked. After the invalid had been lying beside the pool of Bethesda for thirty-eight years, this opportunity was almost beyond his comprehension! Through the power of Christ, he truly was made whole.

Apply — The question has been asked, "If your church closed its doors tomorrow, would your community even know it?" Are we making a daily impact in our community? Consider how your church is collectively meeting the social, spiritual, emotional, and physical needs around you. How are you accomplishing the same as an individual?

Words to Live By

There is need of coming close to the people by personal effort. If less time were given to sermonizing, and more time were spent in personal ministry, greater results would be seen. The poor are to be relieved, the sick cared for, the sorrowing and the bereaved comforted, the ignorant instructed, the inexperienced counseled. We are to weep with those that weep, and rejoice with those that rejoice. Accompanied by the power of persuasion, the power of prayer, the power of the love of God, this work will not, cannot, be without fruit (*The Ministry of Healing*, p. 143).

While He ministered to the poor, Jesus studied also to find ways of reaching the rich. He sought the acquaintance of the wealthy and cultured Pharisee, the Jewish nobleman, and the Roman ruler. He accepted their invitations, attended their feasts, made Himself familiar with their interests and occupations, that He might gain access to their hearts, and reveal to them the imperishable riches (*The Ministry of Healing*, p. 24).

If we would humble ourselves before God, and be kind and courteous and tenderhearted and pitiful, there would be one hundred conversions to the truth where now there is only one (*Testimonies for the Church*, Vol. 9, p. 189).

Weekly Challenge! Start your morning devotional time by praying for divine appointments! Act in faith by carrying Bible tracts or DVDs with you. Remember to keep your eyes open! God will open the door for you to share your faith with others.

"Here Come the Christians," Part Two

In last week's story, two AFCOE students had begun Bible studies with Betsy. Their weekly visits to her drug-infested apartment complex were sometimes unnerving, but the joy on Betsy's face as truth was revealed proved that their efforts were certainly worthwhile.

"Not now, God. We'll see her tonight!" we thought as we tried to drown the still, small voice nagging us all day long. Our AFCOE class was halfway through its prophecy seminar and Betsy was faithfully attending. However, something told us that there was a problem on this night.

"You need to go visit Betsy," the conviction clearly came.

After many attempts at silencing this impression, we finally succumbed. "Fine. We'll go visit her. But what's the point? We'll see her tonight at the seminar!"

At Betsy's door, there was no answer. "We drove all this way for nothing," we sighed, staring absentmindedly at the blue paint peeling off her beat-up door. With every gentle knock, the cracks seemed to spread their wings.

Finally, the door opened, slowly revealing a dark, dark room. "Betsy! What's wrong?" we gasped as she emerged. She looked empty. Broken. Numb. "What happened?" we gently begged.

As Betsy quietly led us into the darkness of her room, she broke down in tears. "I was just sitting in my room trying to decide the best way to take my life," she cried. Her every word shook us to the core. What if we had ignored the convictions of the Holy Spirit and hadn't come?

For the next hour, we cried, prayed, and read promises from God's Word together. Though the devil fought to reclaim Betsy as his own, God prevailed! His gentle, comforting presence was evident that day as Betsy claimed God's promises as her own. Together we knelt, surrendering our lives fully to the One who surrendered His life for us.

A few weeks later, giddy excitement spread throughout the church. Voices sang with passion as baptismal candidates made their way to the front. We couldn't help but imagine that the angels sang a little louder when Betsy climbed into the baptismal tank that Sabbath day. Betsy could think of no greater joy than to follow in the footsteps of Christ and be buried in this watery grave of baptism! Her weathered face shone with pure joy as she emerged from that water to begin a fresh new life in Jesus. As we paused to reflect on how God had miraculously intervened in Betsy's life, we couldn't help but cry tears of joy!

Truly, there is nothing more rewarding than being an ambassador for Christ and witnessing souls being transformed by His love.

Week Three
Our Greatest Need

FOCUS
"This is eternal life, that they may know You, the only true God, and Jesus Christ whom You have sent" (John 17:3).

INTRODUCTION

Have you ever earnestly prayed for revival—yet still felt empty? Maybe you even attended a revival series, and it appeared that everyone around you was being filled with a love for Christ and a passion for ministry, yet you went home feeling empty and saying, *God, why don't I have the joy and the passion that they're experiencing?*

We are often like a water bottle. Imagine taking an empty water bottle over to the sink, turning on the water, and holding it there all day long—*with the cap still fastened tight.* Would the bottle ever be filled?

How often this is true in our spiritual life! Christ longs to fill us with His Spirit! He longs to impart that new life! But He won't force Himself upon us. We must be willing to surrender all that blocks us from a deeper experience with Him.

He was a disciple—casting out demons and healing the sick. He was almost always in the presence of Jesus, sleeping on a mat near Him and eating with Him each day.

Yet Judas was lost! How could that be? How could you be in the very presence of Christ for so long and yet be lost? The answer is found in the book *The Desire of Ages*: "Judas did not come to the point of surrendering himself fully to Christ" (p. 716). Could this chilling statement be said of us?

The most miserable people on earth are not unbelievers but Christians who have surrendered 99 percent to God. They have almost given all, but what they hold back ultimately destroys them. God is asking for 100 percent because He knows this is the only way that we can be truly satisfied.

James Calvert was a missionary to the Fijian Islands in the early 1800s when cannibals inhabited the islands. "You will lose your life and the lives of those with you if you go among such savages," the ship captain fumed. Calvert, a man of great faith, calmly replied, "We died before we came here."

Have you experienced the same? As we commence on this incredible journey of seeking to win souls for Christ, are our own lives fully surrendered to Him? Is there anything blocking us from experiencing the joy of a fully consecrated life?

THIS WEEK IN THE SCRIPTURES

Prayerfully read these passages before beginning this week's study.

- Numbers 22:1–21
- Matthew 25:1–12
- Matthew 8:5–10
- Ephesians 6:11–17
- Proverbs 2:1–5

Absolute Surrender

Read — Numbers 22:1-21

React — What did the Moabites request of Balaam? Do you think Balaam's prayers about it were genuine? What should have been Balaam's final response?

_____

_____

_____

The fear of impending doom filled every heart. No man had stood against them; no country had been left unharmed. Surely they would be no exception, unless an unprecedented plan were devised. King Balak pled of the prophet of God, "Please come at once" and "curse this people for me" (Numbers 22:6). Thus began the story that ultimately led to great apostasy in Israel.

Imagine someone saying to you, "Your child is really annoying me. Can I have your permission to kill her?" As a loving parent, your response would be a resounding "No!" Why then did Balaam ask this of God? Why did he pause to even consider it and pray about it?

How often we pray for wisdom when what we truly need is courage to follow what God has already revealed to us! Charles Spurgeon bemoaned,

> We make up our mind what we are going to do, and often we go down on our knees, and say, "Lord, show me what I ought to do," and then we follow out our intention and say, "I asked God's direction." My dear friend, you did ask it, but you did not follow it; you followed your own. You like God's direction so long as it points you the way you wish to go, but if God's direction led contrary to what you considered your own interest, it might have been a very long while before you had carried it out. But if we in truth and verity do confide in God to guide us, we shall not go far wrong, I know (_The Complete Works of C. H. Spurgeon,_ Vol. 3, Sermons 107–164).

Read — Compare Matthew 7:21-23 with Matthew 25:1-12

React — Why were these professed Christians denied entry? What is the prerequisite for eternal life? Refer also to John 17:3 and 1 Corinthians 8:3.

_____

_____

_____

Excitement was building by the minute. With a rush of activity and squeals of laughter, the bridesmaids hurriedly prepared for the wedding that was to come. While everything else had been prepared, one thing was still missing—the groom.

In Jewish culture, following a proposal, a man would go back and build a room onto his father's house. When this work was completed, he would then go to retrieve his bride. No one knew the exact day or hour—they just knew they had to be prepared when he finally arrived.

Long after the last ray of sunlight touched the horizon, the call was given: "The bridegroom is coming!" Awakened from their sleepy stupor, the darkness of the night revealed some of the bridesmaids' lack of oil. A desperate search for more oil commenced, eventually leading them back to the wedding party and a knock at the host's door. "I do not know you," the heartbreaking words rang out in response.

In a spiritual sense, how could this be? After all, doesn't God know everyone and everything?

Throughout the Bible, the term "know" is used to describe the intimate relationship between man and wife. "Adam *knew* Eve his wife, and she conceived and bore Cain" (Genesis 4:1, emphasis added). This term is frequently used when describing the close, intimate relationship Christ longs to have with us. No mask, no façade—we are fully revealed to the One who knows all—yet He loves us anyway.

However, it is impossible to trust someone we do not know. That would be presumptuous—and dangerous! In the same way, Jesus' prerequisite for entry into heaven is for us to know Him, that is, to have a personal and intimate trust relationship with our God. How can we be sure to experience this relationship as we work to help others have it too?

The Power of Prayer

Read — Deuteronomy 34:10; Daniel 6:10; Matthew 26:36; John 18:2

React — What do these verses have in common? What was of greatest value to these men of faith?

_____

_____

_____

Moses, Daniel, and Jesus—as well as many others, such as Enoch, Abraham, and Nehemiah—these great men of faith had at least one thing in common: they knew the power of prayer! Their daily time with God was the priority of their life and the source of their effectiveness.

In the book *Alone With God*, Matilda Erickson pointedly wrote,

All that men asked of Daniel was that he stop praying for thirty days—just thirty days. Many Christians have stopped praying much longer than that, when the only lions in the way were carelessness and spiritual laziness. But with Daniel it was different. He knew his God. He had met Him alone often. He regarded that appointment with God as the supreme privilege of life—nay, more, an absolute necessity. And he chose rather to be cast into the lions' den with God, than to live in the palace without Him.

Can the same be said of you and your church?

Read — Romans 12:2; Philippians 4:6; Colossians 4:2

React — How do we develop a lifestyle of continual prayer? What should our prayers include?

_____

_____

_____

Prayer is simple enough to be grasped by a child, yet so infinitely deep that grown men must plead, "Lord, teach us to pray" (Luke 11:1). Andrew Murray put it this way:

Jesus never taught His disciples how to preach, only how to pray. ... To know how to speak to God is more than knowing how to speak to man. Not power with men but power with God is the first thing (*The Wisdom of Andrew Murray*, Vol. 1).

Discuss — "Jesus, when preparing for some great trial or some important work, would resort to the solitude of the mountains and spend the night in prayer to His Father. A night of prayer preceded the ordination of the apostles and the Sermon on the Mount, the transfiguration, the agony of the judgment hall and the cross, and the resurrection glory. We, too, must have times set apart for meditation and prayer and for receiving spiritual refreshing. We do not value the power and efficacy of prayer as we should" (*The Ministry of Healing*, p. 509).

Why is it that we don't value the power of prayer as we should? How can we experience a prayer life like Christ's?

_____

_____

_____

Digging Deeper

Read — Matthew 8:5-10

React — Jesus commended the centurion for his great faith. What did the centurion understand that Jesus could do even if not physically present with the ailing servant?

_____

_____

_____

"Only speak a word" (Matthew 8:8), the man of faith begged Him. Though a Roman, he had heard the incredible stories: dead raised, lepers healed, demons cast out. In the face of a humble carpenter, the centurion recognized a man of greater authority than himself.

This same power can be ours today! "The creative energy that called the worlds into existence is in the word of God. This word imparts power; it begets life. Every command is a promise; accepted by the will, received into the soul, it brings with it the life of the Infinite One. It transforms the nature and re-creates the soul in the image of God" (*Education,* p. 126).

Romans 10:17 reminds us that "faith comes by hearing, and hearing by the word of God." As the Word of God is spoken, the same creative power that created the earth recreates our own lives.

Many pray the prayer of the disciples, "Lord, increase our faith." This is well. Yet along with this, it must never be forgotten that faith comes only by the word of God. Therefore, as certainly as your faith shall be increased, it can be only by there being in you an increase of the word of God, and the only way that there can be in you an increase of the word of God, is by your harkening to that word, praying to the Lord for the thing which that word says, depending wholly upon that word for that thing, and thanking him that you have received it. Then and thus that word is received by you, and lives in you (A. T. Jones, *The Review and Herald*, February 28, 1899).

Read — Psalm 119:105; Proverbs 16:20; Acts 17:10, 11

React — Should we ever be content with our knowledge of spiritual things? What must we continue to do?

_____

_____

_____

Engaging in personal Bible study is as essential as eating our daily food. God's Word will sustain and nourish us. What if we constantly prepare food for others (write Bible studies), feed and nourish others (comfort them through prayers and Bible promises), but don't take time to nourish ourselves in prayer and study? It is very easy to fall into the trap of spiritual anorexia—spending our time studying for others while neglecting our own spiritual advancement.

In Ephesians chapter 6, we read about the spiritual soldier clad in the armor of God. But in contrast to Roman soldiers of old, commonly armed with swords, spears, and daggers, this lone spiritual soldier carries but one weapon: the sword of the Spirit. We too have but one weapon. All opinions and experiences break as straw, but the Word of God fails not.

Reflect — "In the Bible we have the unerring counsel of God. Its teachings, practically carried out, will fit men for any position of duty. It is the voice of God speaking every day to the soul" (*Testimonies for the Church*, Vol 4., p. 441).

Discuss — What can we do to continue satisfying our need to go deeper with God?

_____

_____

_____

Pressing In

Read — Luke 24:13–16 and 27–29

React — Why did Jesus not reveal His identity immediately? What would Jesus have done if they had not "constrained" Him?

_____

_____

_____

With heads hung low in grief and confusion, they began their long journey. Lost in their own thoughts, they nearly missed the stranger now in their midst. How easily Jesus could have revealed Himself and brought them the instant relief for which their hearts longed! He could have said, "Look—it's Me! I've risen from the grave!" Instead, Jesus chose to remain hidden while revealing His true character through the Messianic prophecies of old.

Still oblivious to His identity but longing to know more, the disciples pressed the stranger to remain with them. *The Desire of Ages* recorded:

Had the disciples failed to press their invitation, they would not have known that their traveling companion was the risen Lord. Christ never forces His company upon anyone. He interests Himself in those who need Him. Gladly will He enter the humblest home, and cheer the lowliest heart. But if men are too indifferent to think of the heavenly Guest, or ask Him to abide with them, He passes on. Thus many meet with great loss. They do not know Christ any more than did the disciples as He walked with them by the way (p. 800).

How often does the same thing occur in our own lives? Jesus longs to come close, to commune with us, and to reveal Himself through His Word. But unless we invite Him in, He will remain outside the door.

Read — Proverbs 2:1–5

React — Why do people search for gold? How does this analogy compare to our study of the Bible?

_____

_____

_____

"I was not sent except to the lost sheep of the house of Israel," He asserted, the words falling heavy upon her heart. Pressing through the discouragement, she persisted, knowing that He was her only hope. "Lord, help me!" she exclaimed.

Her persistence continued and soon was rewarded, as Jesus publicly praised this woman of faith and healed her ailing daughter. (See Matthew 15:21–28.)

Like Jacob of old, she would not let Jesus go until He blessed her. Christ yearns for this same persistence today! Ellen White shared:

Many, even in their seasons of devotion, fail of receiving the blessing of real communion with God. They are in too great haste. With hurried steps they press through the circle of Christ's loving presence, pausing perhaps a moment within the sacred precincts, but not waiting for counsel. They have no time to remain with the divine Teacher. With their burdens they return to their work. These workers can never attain the highest success until they learn the secret of strength. They must give themselves time to think, to pray, to wait upon God for a renewal of physical, mental, and spiritual power. They need the uplifting influence of His Spirit. Receiving this, they will be quickened by fresh life (*Maranatha*, p. 125).

Tools You Can Use!

Here are five sample activities you can utilize to revitalize your personal devotions. In Bible study, always remember to:

1. **Learn about God, asking ...**
   a. What does this passage teach me about God's love?
   b. What does this passage teach me about God's power?
   c. What does this passage teach me about God's plan?
   d. And simply, what does this passage teach me about God?

2. **Apply the Word to your personal life**
   a. Always pray that God will show you how He wants you to personally respond.
      i. There may be a sin you need to confess.
      ii. There may be something for which to thank God.
      iii. There may be something that you need to make right with another person.
      iv. There may be a whole new career change.
      v. There may be a call to serve.

3. **Keep a journal of it**
   a. Write down what you learned from your time with God.
   b. If you feel especially inspired, write a sermon, short devotional passage, or Bible study based on your studies.
   c. Record the changes you desire God to make in your life.
   d. Record the things for which you are thankful.

4. **Memorize it**
   a. Choose one verse per day or week.
   b. Write the verse on a card in the morning and keep it with you throughout the day.

5. **Share it**
   a. Look for opportunities to share a verse or an inspiring thought with someone during the day.
   b. Verbalizing the verse or thought will help you to remember it.

Apply — Be creative. God wants to have a personal relationship with you. Just as you are unique and special to God, your relationship with Him can be unique and special. No set study pattern works for every person. Find what works for you and apply what you learn.

Words to Live By

Each morning consecrate yourself to God for that day. Surrender all your plans to Him, to be carried out or given up as His providence shall indicate. Thus day by day you may be giving your life into the hands of God, and thus your life will be molded more and more after the life of Christ (*Steps to Christ,* p. 70).

Many are unable to make definite plans for the future. Their life is unsettled. They cannot discern the outcome of affairs, and this often fills them with anxiety and unrest. Let us remember that the life of God's children in this world is a pilgrim life. We have not wisdom to plan our own lives. It is not for us to shape our future. ... Christ in His life on earth made no plans for Himself. He accepted God's plans for Him, and day by day the Father unfolded His plans. So should we depend upon God, that our lives may be the simple outworking of His will. As we commit our ways to Him, He will direct our steps. Too many, in planning for a brilliant future, make an utter failure. Let God plan for you (*The Ministry of Healing,* pp. 478, 479).

Amid the anthems of the celestial choir, God hears the cries of the weakest human being. We pour out our heart's desire in our closets, we breathe a prayer as we walk by the way, and our words reach the throne of the Monarch of the universe. They may be inaudible to any human ear, but they cannot die away into silence, nor can they be lost through the activities of business that are going on. Nothing can drown the soul's desire. It rises above the din of the street, above the confusion of the multitude, to the heavenly courts. It is God to whom we are speaking, and our prayer is heard (*Christ's Object Lessons,* p. 174).

Weekly Challenge! Prayerfully create a devotional plan for the next month. Consider what topic you will study, any areas that you desire to be more intentionally prayerful in, or verses you wish to memorize. Share your plan with a friend and brainstorm additional ways to strengthen your daily walk with Jesus!

In the Caves or in the Clouds, Part One

His hopes were crushed.

As a new Christian, Casano was passionate about his relationship with Christ. He dreamed of attending the Amazing Facts Center of Evangelism (AFCOE) program and learning to share with others the joy he found in Jesus, but it seemed those dearly treasured plans were dashed.

His application had been denied.

Although the staff couldn't help but see Casano's sincerity, they also recognized his limitations. Just three months prior, Cass, as he was affectionately known, had undergone his third operation to remove the last of three brain tumors.

Though only twenty-seven years old, Cass had a patch over one eye and supported himself with a cane. The AFCOE staff, while recognizing his love for Christ, believed he needed to take time to heal before facing the intensity of AFCOE. Regardless, Cass would not be deterred. He knew his time on earth was short. He knew God had saved his life. He knew God was calling him to attend AFCOE. Thus, on registration day, Cass arrived on campus. There was no turning him back!

Staff and students alike were immediately impressed by his sincerity and genuine love for God and people. There was no doubt that this was a converted man. Cass eagerly listened to each class lecture, anxious to learn all he could about reaching his family and friends for Christ. He knew time was of the essence.

A vehement storm was unleashing its fury across the Sacramento Valley. The harder the rains fell, the more fervent the protests against conducting outreach that spring day. Several students gathered to grumble about their fate, when, out of the corner of their eye, they saw a man stand up. With his cane in hand, Cass began to move to the door. "Cass, where are you going?" a voice yelled out.

"I'm going on outreach! Who is going to drive me?" Cass responded with a smile. His dedication to the work, despite the odds, inspired others to do the same.

Continued next week ...

Week Four
The Evangelism Cycle

FOCUS
"Cast your bread upon the waters, for you will find it after many days. ... In the morning sow your seed, and in the evening do not withhold your hand; for you do not know which will prosper, either this or that, or whether both alike will be good" (Ecclesiastes 11:1, 6).

INTRODUCTION
True and lasting success in evangelism demands a definite plan with specific goals. To accomplish this, your church needs a pre-work calendar. This simple tool will help guide the church through the process of preparing for an evangelistic reaping meeting. Having a sure plan will go far in motivating and uniting your church for the evangelistic series. Measurable results are amazingly inspirational!

When Jesus came to save sinners, He caught those sinners' attention in a variety of ways. We are told: "Christ's method alone will give true success in reaching the people. The Savior mingled with men as one who desired their good. He showed His sympathy for them, ministered to their needs, and won their confidence. Then He bade them, 'Follow Me'" (*The Ministry of Healing*, p. 143).

In following the example that Christ set, your church's pre-work calendar needs to have three distinct phases:

- Phase 1: Befriend those in the community
- Phase 2: Minister to needs, win confidence, and strengthen churches
- Phase 3: Invite friends to attend the evangelistic series

Our study this week will provide the tools you need to jumpstart your church to an effective evangelism cycle!

THIS WEEK IN THE SCRIPTURES
Prayerfully read these passages before beginning this week's study.

- Matthew 9:35–38
- Ecclesiastes 11:1–9
- Luke 4:17–21
- John 21:1–8

Phase One

Befriend Those in the Community

Read — 2 Corinthians 9:6; Galatians 6:7; Matthew 9:36–38

React — What must we do before we can expect a harvest? What role does prayer play in this effort?

_____

_____

_____

The goal of this first phase is to create opportunities for church members to interact with people of the community for the purpose of breaking down prejudice and building credibility.

The church members must realize that it is their responsibility to interact with and befriend those attending these bridging events. Make sure that every special event or seminar has an opportunity for church members to mingle with guests and reveal your church's love-filled atmosphere.

Read — Acts 2:46, 47

React — What role did community play in the early church? What was the result of this fellowship and close union?

_____

_____

_____

For many of the new believers, the words of Christ had already rung true: "Now brother will deliver up brother to death, and a father his child; and children will rise up against parents and cause them to be put to death. And you will be hated by all for My name's sake" (Matthew 10:21, 22).

Left without the help of their non-believing biological families, the apostolic church closely united in support, fellowship, and service with one another. "When the Holy Spirit was poured out upon the early church, the brethren loved one another. 'They … did eat their meat with gladness and singleness of heart, praising God, and having favor with all the people: and the Lord added to the church daily such as should be saved.' Those primitive Christians were few in numbers, without wealth or honor, yet they exerted a mighty influence. The light of the world shone out from them" (*Testimonies for the Church*, Vol. 5, p. 239).

Discuss — Read Ecclesiastes 11:1, 6. What do the bread and water represent? What lessons can we apply from these verses to our evangelism efforts?

_____

_____

_____

Phase Two

Minister to Needs, Win Confidence, and Strengthen Churches

Read — Luke 4:18 and Matthew 9:35–38

React — What accompanied the preaching of Christ? How can we apply Christ's method in our communities today?

_____

_____

_____

In the ministry of Christ, preaching was never separated from healing. His eyes were ever open and perceptive to the physical needs around Him. We must make a similar daily impact in our communities.

One useful tool we can utilize is bridge events. As those in the community attend these bridging activities—seminars and ministry outreaches that deal with subjects of community interest, such as health, family, or finance—any prejudice can be broken down. In order for bridge events to run successfully, the outreach leadership team (or personal ministry team) should decide which kind of bridging events will best meet the needs of those in the community and develop a strong team to coordinate these events.

A well-organized plan needs to be implemented to ensure that each guest attending the bridging event is intentionally approached and befriended, possibly by making it the specific goal of every church member to select one or two attendees to personally befriend. This will soften visitors' hearts and win their confidence.

Read — Matthew 14:13, 14

React — Though suffering from His own emotional pain, how did Jesus respond to the multitude? What positive results come from ministering to others, even during our own time of need?

_____

_____

_____

Christ, physically drained from yet another day of ministry, heard the fateful news: John the Baptist had been murdered. Aside from the mother of Christ, no one else understood Jesus' mission as clearly as John did. He was the one who had prepared the way for the Messiah. He was the one who had fearlessly preached God's Word and baptized His beloved Son. And now, he was dead.

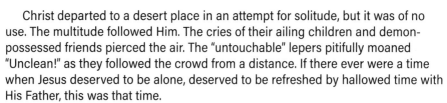

Christ departed to a desert place in an attempt for solitude, but it was of no use. The multitude followed Him. The cries of their ailing children and demon-possessed friends pierced the air. The "untouchable" lepers pitifully moaned "Unclean!" as they followed the crowd from a distance. If there ever were a time when Jesus deserved to be alone, deserved to be refreshed by hallowed time with His Father, this was that time.

But how did Christ respond? He was "moved with compassion" and "healed their sick" (Matthew 14:14). He set aside His own pain, His own exhaustion, and focused solely upon the needs of others. Not only did He minister to their spiritual and emotional needs, He also provided the food they required. Only after they were filled did He depart and enjoy peaceful solitude with His Father.

So often, we use our physical exhaustion, limited resources, or even divisions within our local church as excuses to keep us from ministry. Yet these are the very things that should drive us to it! The life of Christ epitomizes this concept. His nourishment, both physical and emotional, was received through devoted service to others, not from the absence of it. (Read John chapter 4.)

Discuss — What can you and your church do to ensure that not one worker receives an overwhelming workload during your evangelistic cycle?

_____

_____

_____

Phase Three

Invite Friends to Attend the Evangelistic Series

Read — Matthew 13:3–9 and Luke 14:16–23

React — Why is it important to spread the net wide and invite as many people as possible? Will all respond to the call?

_____

_____

_____

Evangelism is similar to a funnel. Initially the funnel is wide, but it quickly narrows in width and capacity. Likewise, there may initially seem to be great community interest in your outreach events, but that interest will narrow as more spiritual truth is revealed. If we desire large results, we must begin with a large funnel of relationships in our communities.

After church members have connected with those in the community, ministered to their needs, and won their confidence, they are then to invite them to attend an evangelistic series.

Members should invite people as personal guests. The goal of the church's pre-work is to get the largest attendance possible for your evangelistic series. If each member can bring one guest, your evangelistic series can be considered a success!

Discuss — "We have an individual accountability to God, an individual work which no one can do for us. It is to make the world better by precept, personal effort, and example. While we should cultivate sociability, let it not be merely for amusement, but for a purpose. There are souls to save" (*The Review and Herald*, November 10, 1885). Here we are warned about creating events merely for the purpose of amusement. Ask yourself: What then is the purpose of facilitating social events for the community? How can we avoid the pitfall of merely entertaining our audience versus ultimately bringing them into a closer relationship with Jesus?

_____

_____

_____

Casting the Net Wide

Read — John 21:3-8

React — What brought about such an incredible catch of fish? Was it the skill of the fishermen?

_____

_____

_____

Times were uncertain. Three and a half years prior, they had willingly left their nets to follow that humble Teacher of truth. In subsequent years, so much had occurred: Demons had been cast out, the sick healed, the dead raised to life, bread multiplied, religious oppression magnified, their Savior brutally executed—and now, *His resurrection.*

Their minds were spinning as they tried to understand what the future might hold. Jesus had always provided for their needs; they had never gone hungry since leaving their occupation as fishermen and following Him. But now what were they to do?

"I am going fishing," Simon Peter finally announced.

Though well trained and experienced, their efforts were fruitless that night. "Cast the net on the right side of the boat, and you will find some," a stranger called out from shore. Though an unreasonable request, these disheartened fishermen cast out their nets once more—and came back with an overwhelming catch. The book *The Desire of Ages* reveals, "Jesus had a purpose in bidding them cast their net on the right side of the ship. On that side He stood upon the shore. That was the side of faith. If they labored in connection with Him—His divine power combining with their human effort—they could not fail of success" (p. 810).

Just as these fishermen felt discouraged when their efforts were fruitless, too often churches are likewise frustrated or bitterly disappointed because their evangelistic meetings seem to fail. Time after time, these disillusioned words have been heard: "Evangelism just doesn't work anymore." But could it be that we aren't casting the net on the right side? Are we truly applying Christ's method of evangelism?

We can know that when human effort, exerted in adequate preparation in the community and in the church, unites with the divine, failure is impossible!

The truth is that public evangelism does work. It is one of the most effective forms of harvest available. However, public evangelism alone seldom works! Often we have overlooked the secret of the harvest: sowing seeds. As your church launches its evangelistic plans, remember the simple biblical principle of sowing and reaping.

Discuss — Read 2 Corinthians 9:6 and Galatians 6:7. Why do we seemingly reap only small harvests? How can they be increased?

_____

_____

_____

Tools You Can Use!

When Jesus came to save sinners, He caught their attention in a variety of ways. Today many thirsty souls don't even know they are longing for the Water of Life. In their search for meaning, they long for health, happy families, financial stability, and other things.

Your bridging programs will help your church minister to these deeply felt needs and are an ideal opportunity to awaken interest in the biblical topics that will be presented in the evangelistic series.

Apply — Here are four important guidelines for bridging events.

1. Short bridging events are best (four to six sessions). Long programs can wear out the church members and tend to overload those attending. You don't want to sap the energy and desire for the evangelistic series! The goal then is to present a short, power-packed program that leaves the participants hungry for more and provides opportunities for church members to create friendships with those attending.

2. Offer bridging events within the two months prior to the start of your evangelistic series. Be sure to include mingling time, when church members can get to know those attending. Encourage members to personally befriend one or two guests, whom they will later invite to the evangelistic series.

3. Choose bridging events the church has done well in the past. Consider the talents and abilities of those within the church leading out in these events, as well as the needs of the community you are trying to reach.

4. The goals of bridging events are to build friendships between church members and guests, meet the needs of the community, and win the guests' confidence. The success of the bridging events can be measured by the number of guests attending and the number of meaningful friendships being developed between members and non-members. Make sure that every guest has a church member assigned to him who will take a personal interest in him and will later invite him to the evangelistic series.

Words to Live By!

Love to man is the earthward manifestation of the love of God. It was to implant this love, to make us children of one family, that the King of glory became one with us. And when His parting words are fulfilled, "Love one another, as I have loved you" (John 15:12); when we love the world as He has loved it, then for us His mission is accomplished. We are fitted for heaven; for we have heaven in our hearts (*The Desire of Ages*, p. 641).

Talk unbelief, and you will have unbelief; but talk faith, and you will have faith. According to the seed sown will be the harvest (*Historical Sketches of the Foreign Missions of the Seventh-day Adventists*, p. 142).

But if you should not live to see it on earth, remember you are only accountable for your labor, and not for your success. Sow still, toil on! "Cast thy bread upon the waters: for thou shalt find it after many days." God will not allow his Word to be wasted; it shall not return unto him void, but shall accomplish that which he pleases (*The Complete Works of C. H. Spurgeon*, Vol. 50, Sermons 2864–2915).

Weekly Challenge! Does your church have an outreach leadership team? If not, work with the pastoral staff to establish one. Work with this team to create a twelve-month evangelism cycle. Delegate event organization and leadership roles among the team in order to effectively employ this cycle. Then watch your church, by the grace of God, become a powerful witness in your community!

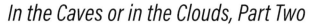

In the Caves or in the Clouds, Part Two

In last week's story, Casano, a twenty-seven-year-old man who had just undergone a third brain surgery to remove tumors, registered to complete the four-month AFCOE course. Though weak from his recent surgeries, Cass' new faith in Christ drove him forward.

Though generally a man of cheerful disposition, during late-night reflections with his roommate, Cass soon revealed fears he carried inside. "What's going to happen someday when we have to run for the mountains? I'm too weak! I can't make it. What will I do?" Cass pled.

His roommate, Michael, assured him, "Brother, when that day comes, I will find you and I will carry you to those caves!" Cass smiled at this guarantee.

Soon the motto of this AFCOE class became: "In the caves or in the clouds." One day soon, I will meet you again—either in the caves awaiting the coming of Christ or in the clouds on that glorious resurrection day. In the caves or in the clouds, I will meet you again.

It wasn't long before those familiar migraines returned. Cass would sit in class, grasping his head with his hands, attempting to endure the pain so he could still soak up every message. Before seeing the physician, he already knew what his diagnosis would be: a fourth brain tumor.

But this time, it was terminal.

After traveling to visit Cass in his hospital room, several students were met by nurses who confessed: "There is something different about this man! I gave my life to Christ because of him." Truly you could sense the presence of angels by his side. Cass refused all pain medications so he could have his mind clear to pray to God and witness to the hospital staff. Regardless of the cost, Cass had chosen the cross.

Just two weeks before his AFCOE graduation, Cass took his last breath. But his short life was certainly not lived in vain; Cass knew his God. He desired nothing else than to please his Savior's heart. He had peace, regardless of the trial, because his eyes were fixed on the cross. Though dead, his testimony lives on— the life of a man sold out for Jesus. Though we will not meet Cass in the caves, by God's grace may we meet again in the clouds on that glorious resurrection day!

Week Five
Friendship Evangelism, Part One

FOCUS

"The harvest truly is plentiful,
but the laborers are few.
Therefore pray the Lord
of the harvest to send out
laborers into His harvest"
(Matthew 9:37, 38).

INTRODUCTION

The sun had risen to full strength by the time her journey began. Its rays beat upon her skin while the weight of her clay water pot pressed hard upon her head, mimicking the heaviness of her heart. She trudged on, lost in thought, as she continued her journey all alone—just how she wanted to be.

To her, the oppressive heat was preferable to the scorching glares she was prone to receive. By this time of the day, no one else would be found at the well; they had long since left from their daily ritual of providing water for their household and, it seemed, endless gossip about the most recent scandal in town— scandals of which she often found herself the center.

Lost in her thoughts, she didn't notice the stranger resting by the well. "Give Me a drink" (John 4:7), the kind voice requested. Glancing at him with surprise, then misguided annoyance, she flippantly replied, "How is it that You, being a Jew, ask a drink from me, a Samaritan woman?" As if He had forgotten, she quickly reminded Him, "For Jews have no dealings with Samaritans" (verse 9).

And yet, in just one brief conversation, Jesus revealed to this disheartened woman her infinite value in the sight of a holy God and the peaceful assurance that the yearnings of her heart could be quenched by His eternal spring of living water. With joy and eager expectation, she ran to those whom she had once avoided, exclaiming with passion, "Come, see a Man who told me all things that I ever did. Could this be the Christ?" (verse 29).

Jesus was a master of reaching the human heart. Regardless of his background, every person walked away feeling respected, loved, and valued by Him.

Jesus saw in every soul one to whom must be given the call to His kingdom. He reached the hearts of the people by going among them as one who desired their good. He sought them in the public streets, in private houses, on the boats, in the synagogue, by the shores of the lake, and at the marriage feast. He met them at their daily vocations, and manifested an interest in their secular affairs. He carried His instruction into the household, bringing families in their own homes under the influence of His divine presence. His strong personal sympathy helped to win hearts (*The Desire of Ages*, p. 151).

Jesus longs for His children to extend this same love to others today! But how do we start these relationships? How can you begin a spiritual conversation with a friend, neighbor, or co-worker? In the following lesson, we will discover some simple tips for making these powerful connections, even for the shyest of believers!

THIS WEEK IN THE SCRIPTURES

Prayerfully read these passages before beginning this week's study.

- Matthew 12:18–21
- Jeremiah 1:4–9
- Exodus 4:10–12
- Matthew 28:16–20
- Mark 10:17–22

Reaching the Heart

Read — Acts 16:16–18

React — Was there anything inaccurate in what this demon-possessed girl said? If not, why was Paul so troubled by her statement?

_____

_____

_____

Even the plain truth, if not revealed in the correct way and at the correct time, can be damaging. We may be sharing all of the truth, but if it is not shared in love, we have ultimately given a false picture of the gospel.

Here is a lesson for all our ministers, colporteurs, and missionary workers. When you meet those, who, like Nathanael, are prejudiced against the truth, *do not urge your peculiar views too strongly*. Talk with them at first of subjects upon which you can agree. Bow with them in prayer, and in humble faith present your petitions at the throne of grace. Both you and they will be brought into a closer connection with heaven, prejudice will be weakened, and it will be easier to reach the heart (*Evangelism*, p. 446, emphasis added).

Read — John 16:12–14

React — Did Jesus reveal everything to His disciples? Why or why not?

_____

_____

_____

Though He longed to share the depths of His knowledge and experience with His followers, Jesus wisely refrained; He knew His disciples were unable to process all that He yearned to share with them.

This principle remains true today. So often, following an evangelistic seminar, newly baptized individuals will excitedly declare, "I can't wait to go home and tell my family all about who the antichrist is!" This well-meaning enthusiasm must quickly be redirected by reminding them of their own journey in truth and of the importance of revealing truth gradually, lest in their zeal they destroy all future witnessing opportunities.

Discuss — How do we know when it is the right time to share a possibly difficult truth with someone? What lessons can we apply from Scripture and from the example of Christ? Consider James 1:5; Matthew 12:18–21; and 2 Timothy 2:23–25.

_____

_____

_____

Unselfish Service

Read — Luke 5:12, 13 and Mark 1:40–42

React — How did Jesus heal this leper? Why did He break this social health rule?

_____

_____

_____

"Unclean ... unclean!" Their mournful shouts echoed throughout the valley. Heads quickly turned in the direction of the pitiful sound, eyes wide with fear. The crowd parted as the Red Sea before them, grown men tripping over themselves in their hasty effort to move away. Mothers quickly pulled their children aside while covering their eyes to hide them from the grotesque sight. But though now hidden from their sight, the overwhelming stench of infected and decaying flesh still filled their nostrils.

Those infected with the terminal illness of leprosy were quickly ushered beyond the city walls. No longer could they visit their families or spend quality time with friends. No longer could they feel the warmth of a loved one's embrace. For the rest of their lives, they would be ostracized, pitied, and lonely. "Unclean!" they must yell to keep at bay those whom they longed to embrace.

Jesus did not have to touch this man in response to his plea for healing; all He had to do was speak a word! Yet Jesus chose to touch him.

From this beautiful example, we see that, while still seeing their physical needs, Jesus did not miss the emotional yearnings of their heart. Jesus touched them, symbolizing the depth of the emotional connection He desires to have with us regardless of our current condition.

How often people come into our churches and all they want is a hug. All they need is to see that someone genuinely loves and cares for them. Are we willing to be the arms of Christ today?

Discuss — Is it possible to do even something good, like evangelism, with selfish motives? What three lessons can we learn from the following passage? "Go to your neighbors one by one, and come close to them till their hearts are warmed by your *unselfish* interest and love" (*Christian Service*, p. 116, emphasis added).

_____

_____

_____

Have you ever met someone with a selfish agenda? He apparently wanted to become friends with you simply because he knew you had the connections to get him the job or relationship that he desired. Did this so-called friendship make you feel loved or valued? Certainly not! And it is the same in evangelism: Do we genuinely love our neighbors and church guests, or are we politely socializing with them only because we want them to go to church and be baptized? Do we care enough to invite them home, or do we offer only a brief welcome at the door? Jesus is calling and empowering us to go much further!

Here are a few simple ways to demonstrate God's love to those around you.

- Bake bread or cookies
- Visit the sick
- Invite a guest at church to your home
- Ask questions, which will reveal your genuine interest in the person
- Listen, listen, listen! (And then listen again)
- Share what God has done for you

Stranger (No) Danger

Read — Jeremiah 1:4-9 and Exodus 4:10-12

React — What is God's response when we are afraid to speak for Him? How did God use these great men of faith? Can He do the same for us today?

_____

_____

_____

For many, the thought of speaking to a stranger is *terrifying*. "What will I say?!" For others, they long to start a spiritual conversation with their co-workers or neighbors but are unsure how to make the transition from a casual discussion.

The acronym FORT—family, occupation, religion, testimony—is an effective and simple approach to get to know others in a way that builds confidence and puts them at ease.

Family: Generally speaking, people love talking about their family! Ask a grandmother about her grandchildren and soon she'll be hauling out a photo album with dozens of sweet stories to share! Asking someone about his family is non-confrontational and an easy way to convey interest, discover needs, and find common ground. Ask questions such as: "Are you originally from this area?" "In what area were you raised?" "Does most of your family live nearby?"

Occupation: Though seemingly stereotypical, it is found that while women often tend toward being more relational and interested in familial conversations, a man's pride and joy often centers in his occupation. If you ask questions about his work or hobbies, cold exteriors often melt away in excitement for an opportunity to share! Listen and then briefly share about areas where you can relate. Consider asking: "What kind of work do you do?" "What type of training is required for this occupation?" "How long have you worked there?" If he is retired, you can ask, "What type of work did you do?" If he is unemployed, ask, "What hobbies do you have?"

Religion: It is helpful to know people's religious background so you can meet them where they are and speak in such a way that they can understand. Make a mental note of similarities and differences in beliefs. Be quick to connect with them on beliefs that you hold in common! Ask questions like: "Do you have a spiritual background?" "Do you find much time to attend a church in this area?" "Have you been [Catholic, Baptist, Muslim, etc.] all of your life?" Notice the way that the second question is *not* phrased: "Do you go to church?" Imagine someone asking you this question with hands on hips and staring you down.

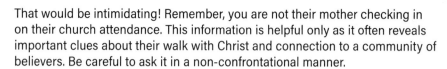

That would be intimidating! Remember, you are not their mother checking in on their church attendance. This information is helpful only as it often reveals important clues about their walk with Christ and connection to a community of believers. Be careful to ask it in a non-confrontational manner.

Testimony: You now have the opportunity to bridge this conversation into a deeper, more personal spiritual conversation. Try to share an aspect of your testimony that will meet any felt needs that your new friends have expressed to you. Demonstrate by sharing your own experience that God can work abundantly in their lives as well. Remember that you are not preaching. Be a friend and genuinely share a short experience about God's working in your life.

FORT is not an interrogation, and it is not a checklist. The goal of this acronym is to provide opportunities to express genuine interest, become aware of felt needs, build relationships, and encourage others through your own love for Christ!

Practice! — Find someone in your group you don't know well and practice FORT! Or better yet, practice FORT this week with a stranger or a co-worker. Record your experience. What went well? What can be improved?

_____

_____

_____

The Fearful Witness

Have you ever been afraid to share your faith? You're not alone! The disciples knew this feeling all too well ...

Read — Matthew 28:16–20

React — What immediately preceded the great commission? How did some of the disciples respond when they saw Jesus?

_____

_____

_____

They doubted? How could this be?! It is seemingly incomprehensible considering these same disciples had been with Jesus as the dead were raised to life, lepers healed, and demons cast out. They had been present when Jesus was beaten, killed, and laid in the tomb. They had heard the good news, "He is risen!" and finally believed the report.

But now they were doubting?

How did Jesus respond to their doubt? Did He banish them to more years of training, or did He voice displeasure at their continual lack of faith? On the contrary, Jesus looked at this group of doubting, dysfunctional men and gave them a mission: "Go and make disciples." You see, it is in the going and making that our faith grows! It is as we step forward in faith that God works miracles on our behalf and our own faith is strengthened as it could be in no other way!

Discuss — What do we have in common with the doubting disciples? Although we have seen God "part the waters" in our lives and work great miracles on our behalf, do we sometimes still doubt Him? What is the remedy for this doubt, as given by Christ?

_____

_____

_____

Read — Mark 10:17–22

React — If someone came to you asking how he could be saved, how would you feel? How did Jesus respond when the rich young ruler walked away?

_____

_____

Pain was evident in His eyes and voice as this wealthy young man, with such great promise, walked away. Jesus had just encountered what many would have described as a divine appointment! Yet it ended in great disappointment.

What if Jesus had said, "Well, I obviously wasn't called into ministry! Look how he walked away." Did Jesus, the greatest Missionary, know what it felt like to have someone He loved walk away from a saving relationship with God? Yes! But thank God that Jesus did not give up in discouragement! Likewise, when the devil tempts us to look at our supposed "failures," let us remember to look to Jesus, find courage in His example, and "let us not grow weary while doing good, for in due season we shall reap if we do not lose heart" (Galatians 6:9).

Tools You Can Use!

We are told "the harvest truly is plentiful, but the laborers are few" (Matthew 9:37). What happens to a ripe harvest if it isn't gathered? It will rot! So also, when we see a spiritual interest, we must gather it! We must not let it rot away.

But on the other hand, how do we minister to green fruit? Do we just disregard them in our search for those who are ready? Imagine you are out in the country picking delicious blueberries. What would happen if you tried to gather berries before they were ripe? Would they ever taste as good? The best decision is to leave them on the vine to ripen and then come back for the harvest!

This illustration applies evangelistically as well. We will indeed encounter green fruit. Rather than forcing religion down someone's throat, we must allow time for him to ripen and then come back to him seeking a harvest. We can encourage him through this ripening process by providing bridging events, a way of making him feel comfortable leaving the security of his comfort zone and entering the premises of a church.

Apply! — Below are a few bridge event ideas you and your church can utilize. Remember to consider the strengths and weaknesses of your church—and how you can use those strengths to further the gospel!

- Cooking school — Give quick, easy, and healthy recipes
- Family life weekend — Strengthen marriage and parenting skills
- Sacred music concert — Provide a suggestions form for each attendee to indicate what he enjoyed, what could be improved, and if he would like special prayer or a visit!
- Dinner with the doctor — A popular way of connecting with the community, offer a free health lecture by a physician at your church and a delicious plant-based meal, followed by free health assessments from medical professionals
- Flea market/community events booth — A very easy and non-scary way to meet people in the community and fulfill their search for a great deal, give away DVDs, magazines, and books, and share testimonies with your church family to inspire others to get involved

Remember to always include extra time for socialization so that church members can connect with guests from the community.

But wait! There's more! The possibilities are endless ...

- Financial seminars
- Stop smoking classes
- Depression recovery sessions
- Nursing home ministries

- GED programs
- English classes
- Free guitar or other instrument classes
- Bake gift loaves of bread for visitors
- Advertise free Bible studies in your paper or online

Be sure to post a church advertisement in the newspaper. Promote everything in your church to the community!

Words to Live By

Jesus, dwelling in you, desires to speak to the hearts of those who are not acquainted with Him (*Steps to Christ*, p. 115).

The heart that rests most fully upon Christ will be most earnest and active in labor for Him (*Steps to Christ*, p. 33).

It is the duty of every Christian to be Christ to his neighbor (Martin Luther).

The Lord God of Israel is watching every worker, to see whether he is in earnest, whether he carries upon his heart the burden of souls. God sees whether his servants touch these living interests with the ends of their fingers, or whether they grasp them with all their might. If all had the interest that Knox felt when he cried, "Give me Scotland, or I die!"—a wrestling with God that will not be denied—the Lord would work with their efforts, and would give them souls for their hire. They would not be lifted up because of their success, nor would they for a moment fear that someone else would receive the credit due to them; but they would be so grateful to God for the souls saved that his praise would be in their hearts and on their lips day and night. It is such workers that God will make mighty in his cause (*Gospel Workers,* p. 297).

Weekly Challenge! This week meet two new families in your neighborhood or deepen pre-existing relationships with families on your street. Bake them a loaf of bread, bring them cookies, invite them to your home for dinner, or visit one of their loved ones who is ill. Pray for ways that God can use you to reach their hearts, look for opportunities to share your quick testimony, and seek to minister to their needs. Be intentional about doing so, starting this very week! Imagine how quickly the gospel could go to the ends of the earth if every Christian home were a mission center. Let that light shine brightly for Jesus this week!

Truth at All Cost

A story from Pastor Doug Batchelor

Born into a tight-knit Amish community, Andy and his wife, Naomi, had been taught the Ten Commandments since their childhood. But Andy had always wrestled with the question of why the Amish did not keep the fourth commandment. He also had suffered much conflict over the question of why a God of love would cause people to suffer in hell forever. These unanswered questions nagged at his heart.

One day his brother approached him with a strange magazine that he had received from a Sabbath-keeping neighbor. They quickly began to compare the *Daniel and Revelation* magazine with the Bible and were shocked to discover that its teachings were true! Later, the neighbor shared a copy of *The Desire of Ages.* The book caused Andy to think deeply, and he says he spent long periods of time pondering these truths that were both wonderful and challenging. Then he received *The Great Controversy.* "When I read that book, there was no question in my mind that it was inspired."

"I would stay awake at night and think about these things," Andy says. "When I read the Amazing Facts magazine, I came to understand the truth." Andy shares that it was a joy and relief to discover answers to questions he had struggled with for so long. But it was also a challenge to think about what would happen if he took a stand. Finally, though, conviction won. "I realized I was living a lie, and I could not do that."

Naomi, who was studying with her husband, saw the truth as well. She had questions regarding what she felt was a conflict between two of the commandments: the fourth and the fifth. "I had understood the fifth commandment to mean that honoring our parents means to always *obey* them," she explains. "I couldn't see how I could go forward in keeping the fourth commandment when it would mean disobeying my parents." Naomi's mother was living with their family at the time, and Naomi worried what would happen with her mom if they went forward in their new understanding of Bible truth. "Andy helped me understand that I could obey God and still respect my mom. Then I was able to make my decision to go forward. It was a struggle, but it was worth it. We see more blessings as we continue in His light."

Andy believes that it is the strong moral principles that he and Naomi were taught in the Amish religion that actually ended up giving them the strength to finally leave it.

Determined to help the Amish learn the Bible messages from which they had gained so much joy, Andy and Naomi have started a ministry in Ohio. They and their seven children, aged one to ten, are determined to remain as lights among the Amish community. Through friendship evangelism and sharing literature, their efforts are already making an impact!

And it all began with a neighbor sharing an Amazing Facts magazine ...

Week Six
Friendship Evangelism, Part Two

FOCUS
"They overcame him by the blood of the Lamb and by the word of their testimony, and they did not love their lives to the death" (Revelation 12:11).

INTRODUCTION

He could hardly contain his excitement. Long before the rooster crowed, his bare feet slid to the cool floor and he rushed out his bedroom door. There was nothing more exciting for the little boy than a whole summer filled with laughter on his grandparents' farm!

"Grandpa, what does Grandma read every morning?" the boy with the sun-kissed face inquired.

"She's reading the story of Calvary," came the warm response.

A weatherworn hand tousled his hair. "But Grandpa, if she's reading the same story every morning, why does she still cry?"

"Well, son, it's because she truly believes it!"

Though the gospel was written down many years ago, the impact of the Calvary story remains fresh. As it is retold and experienced in our lives, it cannot help but make an impression on all who come within our reach. Our personal testimony, our experience with Jesus, is the most powerful sermon ever preached!

People enjoy stories, especially when they are the experience of the storyteller. Your personal conversion, when shared effectively, will often awaken the realization of deep spiritual needs in your listeners and naturally lead them to want to know more about the power of the gospel.

But what do we share? If you were raised a Christian, you may wonder if you even *have* a testimony. On the other hand, how can twenty or thirty or sixty years' worth of testimonies be condensed into a three-minute conversation? Without a doubt, your testimony is a story that many are craving to hear! In the following study, we will learn how to more effectively share the joy we have experienced in Christ.

THIS WEEK IN THE SCRIPTURES

Prayerfully read these passages before beginning this week's study.

- 1 John 1:1–4
- Acts 26:4–23
- Joshua 4:1–8
- Philippians 4:4, 6, 7

Heaven's Chosen Agency

Read — 1 John 1:1–4

React — What should we declare? According to this passage, why should we share our testimony with others?

_____

_____

_____

People can argue with your theology. They can contradict your interpretation of the Bible. They can ridicule your faith. But they cannot challenge the power of your testimony. God's transforming work in the lives of individuals is the most compelling evidence of His existence. A life that is melted and molded under the influence of the Holy Spirit is an evangelistic sermon all on its own.

Our confession of His faithfulness is Heaven's chosen agency for revealing Christ to the world. We are to acknowledge His grace as made known through the holy men of old; but that which will be most effectual is the testimony of our own experience. We are witnesses for God as we reveal in ourselves the working of a power that is divine. Every individual has a life distinct from all others, and an experience differing essentially from theirs. God desires that our praise shall ascend to Him, marked by our own individuality. These precious acknowledgments to the praise of the glory of His grace, when supported by a Christ-like life, have an irresistible power that works for the salvation of souls (*The Desire of Ages*, p. 347).

Read — Matthew 10:32, 33 and Revelation 12:11

React — What role does active witnessing play in our salvation? How does our testimony empower us to be overcomers?

_____

_____

_____

Many people mistakenly speak of the "silent witness" as the only way to convince others about Jesus. While our characters are, indeed, a silent testimony to our conversion, we are not to give God a backseat. He is not content to have us silently acknowledge Him as if He were some lucky horseshoe hanging above the fireplace. Jesus said, "Whoever confesses Me before men, him I will also confess before My Father who is in heaven. But whoever denies Me before men, him I will also deny before My Father who is in heaven" (Matthew 10:32, 33).

Our conversations are opportunities to lift up Jesus. As we begin to tell others of His wonderful grace at work in our lives, we are transformed into messengers of mercy. People will see the light of His love in our eyes and they will long for the experience of which we speak. Even better, God has promised to give us the words to speak!

69

Paul's Golden Opportunity

The Bible gives us many examples of those who shared their personal witness in a convincing and compelling manner. One of the most powerful is recorded in Acts 26. When the apostle Paul stood before King Agrippa, he spoke simply, logically, and clearly about his life before salvation, how he met Christ, and what his life was like after conversion.

Read — Acts 26:4–23

React — When given time to speak in his defense, what did Paul share? How did King Agrippa respond to this stirring message?

_____

_____

_____

Suffocating silence filled the air. Every sound was hushed as all ears strained to hear the words of the accused. "You are permitted to speak for yourself" (Acts 26:1), King Agrippa assured him. All eyes turned to the aged prisoner whose dignified bearing still commanded respect. With clarity in his voice and sincerity in his eyes, Paul began to tell the story of his devoted youth in the strictest sect of Pharisaism, of his passionate rage against the followers of Christ, of being struck blind as the voice of the Persecuted One rang from the heavens, of his present joy in winning souls for Christ. All the while, King Agrippa sat spellbound, captivated by every word. "You almost persuade me to become a Christian" (Acts 26:28), he loudly exclaimed, lost in a moment of passion as his heart cried out for the same freedom experienced by the prisoner chained before him.

Paul had been given a golden opportunity. Here was his chance to beg King Agrippa for deliverance or to plead the cause of the innocent. He could have preached of the Messianic prophecies fulfilled or of the eternal kingdom that was to come. Yet Paul, led by the Holy Spirit, spoke an even deeper message, a message that could bring a king to his knees. In this golden moment, Paul shared his personal testimony.

Discuss — The testimony of Paul can be readily divided into three sections: his life before meeting Jesus (verses 4, 5, 9-11), his conversion experience (verses 12-18), and his life after his conversion (verses 19-23). What three lessons can we learn from the way in which Paul shared?

_____

_____

_____

Nothing to Fear

Read — Joshua 4:1–8

React — *After the miraculous crossing of the Jordan River, what did Joshua command the people to do? Why did the Lord instruct them to do this?*

_____

_____

_____

As with the Israelites of old, we are likewise counseled to remember our testimony. "In reviewing our past history, having traveled over every step of advance to our present standing, I can say, Praise God! As I see what God has wrought, I am filled with astonishment, and with confidence in Christ as leader. *We have nothing to fear for the future, except as we shall forget the way the Lord has led us, and His teaching in our past history*" (*Christian Experience and Teachings of Ellen G. White,* p. 204, emphasis added).

We can readily apply the apostle Paul's model for sharing his testimony. Using his three-category method allows us to be more succinct, prevents us from wearing out our audience, and allows us to focus on what is most relevant.

Your Past:

- What things were most important to you? What did your life revolve around?
- Why were they so important? What basic need were you attempting to fulfill?
- How did you try to satisfy that need?

How You Found Jesus:

- When did you first hear the message of Christ? What was your reaction?
- If you were raised in a Christian home, when did it become your own personal experience? Was there a dark time or trial you endured that brought you closer to Jesus?

Your Life Now in Christ:

- How did Jesus specifically satisfy the basic needs you had before you found Him?
- What changes have occurred in your life as a result?
- How do you know Christ is in your life?

Share! Write out your testimony, using three to four sentences per section, and share it with someone in your small group.

Rejoice Always!

Read — Philippians 4:4, 6, 7

React — Is this a realistic statement? In what ways did Paul exemplify this passage in his own life?

_____

_____

_____

"Oh, I know exactly how you feel!"

"Just get over it. After all, I did!"

We've all heard these less-than-comforting statements. More often than not, we instinctively cringe with frustration. "How could you really understand?" we mutter. Advice is so easy to give but often difficult to swallow.

At first glance, the apostle Paul was no exception. "Rejoice in the Lord always" (Philippians 4:4), he instructed the fledgling Philippian believers. These devoted Christians understood persecution. Their meager belongings and even their lives were often at risk for their faith. "How could Paul tell them to always rejoice, even when enduring such great trials?" we might ask.

But any Philippian believers tempted to doubt his credibility could recall Paul's personal testimony. After receiving a stirring vision to come over to Macedonia, Paul immediately set sail and landed in the territory of Philippi. But all was not chocolate and roses; rather, he was met with fierce persecution, beaten with rods, and thrown mercilessly into a cold, damp jail cell. Surely Paul had reason to complain! But what was his response?

He prayed and sang to God! Even in his darkest moment, Paul lifted his voice in praise. His own example confirmed his words, "Rejoice in the Lord always. Again I will say, rejoice!" (Philippians 4:4).

Read — 2 Corinthians 1:3, 4

React — *What should we share in order to bring comfort to others? What does this text teach us about the importance of sharing our testimony?*

_____

_____

_____

We might be tempted at times to feel as though our testimony isn't that important or interesting; or maybe we are ashamed of things in the past and we'd rather keep them hidden under the rug of time. But this passage reminds us that God has brought healing into our lives so that we can offer the same healing to others in their time of need!

There is nothing sweeter than the presence of a friend who can truly understand our pain and share healing received in Christ!

Tools You Can Use!

Apply! — Here are a few simple tips to strengthen your testimony.

1. Learn to tell what God has done, not what you have done. Be humble.

2. Use terms people can understand. Imagine saying, "I've been washed by the blood of the Lamb" to an atheist who has had no exposure to Christianity; he would picture a rather gruesome sight! Talk in such a way that your listeners can relate. Consider using phrases like, "My life is so much more peaceful now;" "I'm much more confident now that I'm not carrying all this guilt with me;" and, "Life is much more manageable when I remember that God has a plan for me."

3. Be realistic. Share how Christ enables you to walk through your problems, rather than removing them from your life.

4. Don't be critical of other people or churches. Your former church persuasion may not have been doctrinally correct, but we must remember that we were once a part of them.

5. Never glamorize sin. Be very careful in giving details of the evils of your past. Instead, give details about your new life. Though stories of the past can help you relate, never forget that Christ is and must be the center of your testimony.

6. Instead of dwelling on the trials and sacrifices, dwell on the blessings and rewards.

7. Don't be too religious or preachy! Rather, sound conversational and use informal language.

8. Identify with your audience. Tailor your testimony to meet them.

9. Build your testimony around a theme. Choose something characteristic of your experience that is of general interest to non-Christians; e.g., success, search for meaning and purpose, dealing with tragedy, etc.

10. *Pray* each day that God will make you aware of someone who needs to hear your testimony. Keep alert; He will show you the person.

Remember, the purpose of preparing your testimony is not necessarily to memorize it and give it verbatim, but to help you put into words some of the important and interesting details of your conversion and personal relationship with Jesus. A testimony serves primarily as a "door opener," not a "convincing tool."

Words to Live By

As witnesses for Christ, we are to tell what we know, what we ourselves have seen and heard and felt. ... We can tell how we have tested His promise, and found the promise true. We can bear witness to what we have known of the grace of Christ. This is the witness for which our Lord calls, and for want of which the world is perishing (*The Desire of Ages*, p. 340).

"Ye shall be witnesses unto Me" (Acts 1:8). These words of Jesus have lost none of their force. Our Savior calls for faithful witnesses in these days of religious formalism; but how few, even among the professed ambassadors for Christ, are ready to give a faithful, personal testimony for their Master! Many can tell what the great and good men of generations past have done, and dared, and suffered, and enjoyed. They become eloquent in setting forth the power of the gospel, which has enabled others to rejoice in trying conflicts, and to stand firm against fierce temptations. But while so earnest in bringing forward other Christians as witnesses for Jesus, they seem to have no fresh, timely experience of their own to relate. ...

Without a living faith in Christ as a personal Savior, it is impossible to make your faith felt in a skeptical world. If you would draw sinners out of the swift-running current, your own feet must not stand on slippery places. ...

We need constantly a fresh revelation of Christ, a daily experience that harmonizes with His teachings. High and holy attainments are within our reach. Continual progress in knowledge and virtue is God's purpose for us. His law is the echo of His own voice, giving to all the invitation, "Come up higher; be holy, holier still" (*Gospel Workers*, pp. 273, 274).

Weekly Challenge! Write out your testimony using the principles shared this week. The more you practice sharing your personal experience, the more natural sharing it with others will become!

This week, pray and ask God to reveal someone with whom you can share your testimony. It may be at work, or on an airplane, or simply with a discouraged friend. Move forward in faith! God will open the door when we seek to be living witnesses for Him.

Answering the Call, Part One

Shots rang out, startling him from his moment of reprieve. With gun in hand, Jerrod dove headlong under the cover of an armored vehicle—with not a moment to lose. Mortar shells poured down from the sky, decimating everything within reach. Chaos reigned as soldiers frantically scrambled for cover, their shouts and artillery fire piercing the cloudless night.

Chocolate and roses were far from Jerrod's mind on this Valentine's Day. All he could hope for was to survive to see the sunshine of another blistering day.

No one could have foretold the journey that this small-town boy would make. Raised in rural Wyoming, Iraq was the last place he would have ever imagined himself. And yet, no aspect of his life had ever been conventional.

At a young age, Jerrod felt the call to ministry. He took his catechism classes very seriously and prided himself in being a devout Catholic. One afternoon, he excitedly informed his stepfather that someday he would be a priest! "You know that priests can't get married, right?" his stepfather replied. This discovery immediately quenched all desire for the priesthood. It wasn't long before he took a far less pious path.

After a childhood littered with verbal and physical abuse, Jerrod craved acceptance at any cost. Drugs, gangs, and violence became avenues to numb his deep pain. But they weren't enough. They couldn't bring the relief he craved. Soon his path turned once again to religion in a desperate attempt for peace. A friend's invitation led him to a small country church and an intriguing message. He sat spellbound night after night as an Amazing Facts evangelist revealed the answers and genuine acceptance he had craved all his life—and he could not resist. The love of Christ overwhelmed Jerrod with joy as he stepped into a new life through baptism.

Once again Jerrod pursued ministry, but this time with his bride! But the financial burden of caring for a family and paying for tuition soon engulfed him. His zeal for God waned. Out of desperation, Jerrod enlisted in the military. This decision would impact his life forever.

Long days were passed at basic training under the scorching Oklahoma sun. His specialization in field artillery soon led him to his next station: Kuwait. Driving convoys through the desert was never without risk. One particularly hot day found his the lead vehicle in a convoy. Wind whipped the dust around them as he and his fellow soldiers searched the horizon for danger.

Suddenly the ground shook with violent intensity. Thrown from their seats, they peered through the smoke for the enemy. Smoldering ruins revealed a bone-chilling sight: a bomb's fierce explosion had destroyed the armored vehicle immediately behind him. Jerrod knew without a doubt that the hand of God had protected him from certain death.

Continued next week ...

Week Seven
Giving Bible Studies, Part One

FOCUS
"Beginning at Moses and all the Prophets, He expounded to them in all the Scriptures the things concerning Himself" (Luke 24:27).

INTRODUCTION

As fun as it had been, the family was ready for this road trip to be over. There was just no place like home! That, compounded with the fact that there were no healthy options on the breakfast menu that morning, left them anxious to get on their way.

After finally settling upon their order, the family chatted happily with the waitress and with one another during their meal. Now with their bill paid, they began to depart quickly from the restaurant. Suddenly, the daughter stopped and began rummaging around in her oversized purse. "What are you looking for?" the mother inquired, anxious to depart.

"I don't know why, but I just feel like we should leave a Bible tract behind. I can't seem to find one!" she replied as her search continued into a deep recess of her purse. Finally, with a smile of triumph stretched across her face, she brought out a rather wrinkled pamphlet entitled, "Where Is God When I'm Hurting?" Stuffing several dollars inside to improve its disheveled appearance before leaving it on the table, mother and daughter began to walk out to join the rest of the family.

Suddenly a voice yelled out. "Wait! Stop!" Puzzled, the family quickly turned around as their waitress rushed over to them, the tract held up high in her hand. "Can I ask you a question?" she pled. "How did you know that I was hurting?"

Though unseen to them, God knew that this smiling waitress was carrying a heavy heart. Because of one little sharing tract, a door was opened to share the hope and healing that is found in Jesus! With hands grasped, the family and the waitress formed a circle to pray in the parking lot. The presence of other customers walking by went unnoticed by the waitress as tears of joy and relief streamed down her face.

We are told:

There are many who are reading the Scriptures who cannot understand their true import. All over the world men and women are looking wistfully to heaven. Prayers and tears and inquiries go up from souls longing for light, for grace, for the Holy Spirit. Many are on the verge of the kingdom, waiting only to be gathered in (*Acts of the Apostles,* p. 109).

God is calling us to be the answer to their prayers! With Bible in hand, we can bring the message of hope that others are longing to hear! This week's lesson will begin equipping us to give more powerful and Christ-centered Bible studies.

THIS WEEK IN THE SCRIPTURES
Prayerfully read these passages before beginning this week's study.

- 2 Timothy 4:1, 2
- Luke 24:13–35
- Acts 8:26–38
- Isaiah 46:9, 10
- John 9:1–25
- Mark 5:1–20

Perennial Christians

Read — 2 Timothy 4:1, 2

React — What did Paul charge Timothy to do? Can we ever take a day off from sharing the Word?

_____

_____

_____

Like Timothy of old, we as modern disciples must be ready at all times to share the beauty of God's Word with others. Our eyes must always be open so we don't miss the divine appointments before us!

Discuss — Where should we begin to look for people who might be interested in starting Bible studies with us? Consider the following options and then discuss as a group where you personally will begin.

1. *Utilize the church visitor list.* That big book in the foyer wasn't created as an autograph collection! Personally visit the guests, bringing a book or freshly made loaf of bread. Invite them to begin Bible studies or to attend other church functions that they might be interested in (vacation Bible school, concerts, healthy cooking programs, etc.).

2. *Missing members.* Visit missing members, build relationships, and invite them to attend special church functions. Remember that former members may already be quite familiar with doctrinal studies. Consider using Bible studies that are more relationship oriented and which encourage them to begin or strengthen their own personal devotions.

3. *Youth in the church.* Never underestimate the power of youth ministry! Jesus was twelve when He began to publically share the Bible—even with church leaders! Our youth are equally capable of understanding and sharing the Word of God today. These most pivotal years must be used to encourage them into a lasting relationship with Jesus.

4. *Spouses or family of established church members.* Who is in our circle of influence? Are there visitors who grudgingly attend church with their believing spouse, yet have never had an opportunity to study these truths for themselves? Prayerfully build your relationship with them and look for opportunities to invite them to attend a small group Bible study or a one-on-one study with you.

5. *Door-to-door outreach.* Never underestimate the power of door-to-door evangelism! Use surveys, share flyers for upcoming health events, or just bring your youth group along and offer prayers for the people in your neighborhood, leaving Bible tracts behind as a "free gift."

6. *Individuals who have gone through a previous series.* Perhaps you have had a prophecy seminar, or even a family or health seminar, in the past, but for one reason or another, guests quit attending. Follow up with these contacts. At one point they had a strong enough spiritual interest to attend! Continue to nurture that relationship with them, answer any Bible questions, and invite them to begin weekly Bible studies.

7. *Media interests.* Contact local media programs, such as Amazing Facts, and ask if they have any Bible school or media interests in your community. If so, visit these individuals as a local representative for that ministry, asking them how they've been enjoying the material and if they have any questions. As you build this relationship with them, you'll have the opportunity to then offer Bible studies.

8. *Summer canvassing programs.* A literature evangelist gathers Bible study leads all summer long and then hands them over to the local church, hoping and praying that someone might just follow them up. But these leads are gold! All the hard work has been done for us! Take the initiative to ask your pastor or conference to host a canvassing program in your community. Train a team to assist you in following up leads.

Prophecy's Core

Read — Luke 24:13–16, 25–27, 32 and Acts 8:26–38

React — Who was presented as the center of these Bible studies? When the listeners saw Jesus revealed through prophecy, what was their response? How can we apply this approach today?

_____

_____

_____

Jesus is, and must be, the center of every Bible study! A knowledge of the truth without a genuine love for Christ is the recipe for Pharisaism.

Notice Christ's approach in encouraging these disheartened believers: Rather than simply revealing His identity to them, Jesus began this Bible study in the books of Moses and all the prophets; His study was comprehensive, demonstrating the value of the entirety of the Scriptures. The Bible also records that He "expounded to them in all the Scriptures the things concerning Himself" (Luke 24:27). In other words, Jesus is the center of the Bible. Regardless of what you study, from the sanctuary to the rock in the wilderness to the temple cornerstone to the lives of Abraham or David, the character and identity of Jesus is revealed.

Discuss — Often, prophecy is used to interest the community in attending church seminars. Why is this done? What are the benefits? Are there any words of caution to keep in mind?

_____

_____

_____

When the word "Revelation" is spoken, what comes to mind? The antichrist? Armageddon? Beasts? Tribulation? Yet Revelation 1:1 reminds us that this incredible book is a "Revelation of Jesus Christ"! It is a revealing of the Lamb, slain from the foundation of the world. A Revelation seminar that is not saturated in the love and character of Christ is an inaccurate interpretation of the Scriptures! It is only as Christ is lifted up that people are drawn to Him (John 12:32).

So why use prophecy?

First, prophecy reveals the Lamb and prepares us to face the future with hope. Second, there is a great interest in studying prophecy but very few churches offer information on this topic! This curiosity can be used to create larger community involvement. And third, prophecy was given to increase our own confidence in the inspiration of the Bible, and consequently, its personal application to our lives today!

Read — John 14:29 and Isaiah 46:9, 10

React — What do these verses teach us about the importance of studying prophecy? As we near the end of time, should our interest in prophecy increase or decrease?

_____

_____

_____

The ABCs of Giving Bible Studies

Read — 2 Timothy 2:15

React — The Greek word *orthotomeo*, translated as "rightly divide," means to teach the truth directly and correctly. If there is a right way to handle and teach the truth, is there a wrong way? According to this passage, how concerned should we be with presenting truth correctly?

_____

_____

_____

Three principles help us remain grounded in our personal study and presentation of the Scriptures to others:

A. *Always present Jesus first!*
   The very first and the most important thing is to melt and subdue the soul by presenting our Lord Jesus Christ as the sinbearer, the sin-pardoning Saviour, making the gospel as clear as possible (*Evangelism*, p. 264).

   The wonderful love of Christ will melt and subdue hearts, when the mere reiteration of doctrines would accomplish nothing (*The Desire of Ages*, p. 826).

B. *Reveal truth gradually.*
   The path of the just is like the shining sun, that shines ever brighter unto the perfect day (Proverbs 4:18).

   I still have many things to say to you, but you cannot bear them now (John 16:12).

C. *Make regular appeals.*
   At the close of every meeting [and Bible study], decisions should be called for (*Testimonies for the Church*, Vol. 6, p. 64).

   Choose for yourselves *this day* whom you will serve. ... But as for me and my house, we will serve the LORD (Joshua 24:15, emphasis added).

Read — Bring earnestness and fervency into your prayers, and into your Bible readings ... that you may leave the impression that the sacred truths you are presenting to others are to you a living reality. Whatever you do for Jesus, seek with all your powers to do it with earnestness. Never feel that you have attained to the highest point, and can therefore rise no higher. ... Seize the most interesting portions of Scripture that you can bring before them, come right to the point, and seek to fasten their attention, and instruct them in the ways of the Lord (*The Review and Herald*, July 26, 1887).

React — From this passage, we can learn at least five points on how to give effective Bible studies:

1. Be earnest
2. Be genuine (living reality)
3. Be committed
4. Be teachable
5. Be interesting

Discuss — How can each of these principles be applied? Below, record which principle(s) you are weaker in and practical steps on how this can be improved in your Bible studies.

_____

_____

_____

Sharing Is Caring

Read — John 9:1-11, 24, 25 and Mark 5:18-20

React — What do these two stories have in common? Did either of these men receive lengthy training in soul winning? Yet what occurred immediately following their healing/conversion?

_____

_____

_____

Their eyes narrowed in anger as they spat the words out of their mouths, "This man is not from God!" With firm conviction, the humble reply came, "Whether He is a sinner or not I do not know. One thing I know: that though I was blind, now I see" (John 9:25).

Often the fear that our knowledge is limited keeps us from sharing our faith. In stark contrast to us, two men who had spent a relatively short amount of time with Jesus turned their cities upside down for Him as they fearlessly proclaimed their faith. They did not know much, but this much they knew: Jesus had set them free!

The book _Christ's Object Lessons_ reminds us, "He who begins with a little knowledge, in a humble way, and tells what he knows, while seeking diligently for further knowledge, will find the whole heavenly treasure awaiting his demand. The more he seeks to impart light, the more light he will receive. The more one tries to explain the Word of God to others, with a love for souls, the plainer it becomes to himself" (p. 354).

Consider — Sometimes we feel as though our efforts are so pitifully small. "What can I, a lowly church member, do to make a significant impact in my community?" But pause to consider the chart below, which appears in the book _Winsome Witnessing_ by Gary Gibbs.

After ...	Gifted evangelist wins 1,000 converts a day	Believers win just one person a year
1 year ...	365,000	2
2 years ...	730,000	4
3 years ...	1,095,000	8
4 years ...	1,460,000	16
5 years ...	1,825,000	32
8 years ...	2,920,000	256
23 years ...	8,395,000	8,388,608
24 years ...	8,760,000	16,777,216
25 years ...	9,125,000	33,554,432

Notice: In year 24, individuals had reached nearly twice that of the professional evangelist. In year twenty-five, it's nearly four times as many—so long as each new believer commits to winning one soul every year.

Imagine if this were occurring in our churches today! The same God who multiplied the loaves and the fishes can multiply our efforts as we seek to remain faithful in what is least.

Discuss — There are many ways to invite our friends to begin Bible studies with us! Consider the two options below and practice them in your small group!

"You and I were recently discussing why there is so much pain in this world if God is a God of love. I found this great set of Bible studies that answers this question and so many more! What do you think about checking them out together this Wednesday for about thirty minutes? I think you'll really enjoy them."

Note: *What topics have you discussed recently? Terrorism? Prophecy? What happens after death? Use any item of interest in these lessons to pique their curiosity.*

"I'm taking this class on how to give Bible studies. The first study talks about whether the Bible can be trusted. I'm supposed to practice my Bible study on someone. It'll take only about thirty to forty-five minutes, and I know you'll enjoy the lesson! Could you do me a favor and let me practice my study on you?"

Note: *Does this really work? The answer is Yes! We have heard testimony after testimony (and have experienced it ourselves) of how God has used these simple canvasses to open the door to share His Word and lead others into a saving relationship with Jesus. Watch God work today!*

Tools You Can Use!

As the saying goes, why reinvent the wheel? There are many powerful Bible studies in circulation today. But these studies often lack an emphasis on a personal relationship with Christ—or they may be too dry and uninteresting for audiences today.

Take one of these Bible studies, study it thoroughly yourself, and then add the following components to your study plan to make it more Christ-centered, relevant, personable, and interesting:

- Introduction
- Three main points (spread throughout the study)
- Two illustrations and one personal testimony (to illustrate/elaborate on your main point)
- Diagnostic questions (to be discussed in Week Eight's lesson)
- Summary
- Appeal
- Decision question

Apply! — Here is an expansion of the points above:

1. Three main points

    a. What are the three most important things you want the person to remember?

    b. Each point should be two sentences long. The first sentence is your main thought and the second one is the personal application.

    c. At the end of your Bible study, review these points with your study interest (Summary). Doing this will refresh his memory before you ask him to make a decision.

    d. Example: Daniel's devotion to prayer was his strength, even during the most dangerous of times. When we face challenges in life, we can rest assured that the God of Daniel will still answer our prayers today.

2. Illustrations

    a. You can use a story, an amazing fact, or anything else that will help him understand and remember the point you are trying to make. Make sure that the illustration explains and bolsters that main point.

    b. Christ masterfully wove illustrations into all of His conversations. For years to come, the passerby would stop to ponder His lesson as he walked by the lillies of the field or watched a man sowing his field. "In His teaching, Christ drew His illustrations from the great treasury of household ties and affections, and from nature. The unknown was illustrated by the known; sacred and divine truths, by natural, earthly things, with which the people were most familiar. These were the things that would speak to their hearts, and make the deepest impression on their minds" (*Counsels to Parents, Teachers, and Students*, p. 178).

c. Other sources for illustrations: personal experience, stories from books or from the news, stories of heroes of faith, interesting nature or science facts, and illustrations you have heard others use—it's quite likely they also borrowed them!

d. Remember that illustrations are key. They can make or break a Bible study. Be intentional about finding good illustrations that will clearly explain your main point and be relevant to your audience.

3. Personal testimony

a. Use a short story about how God has worked in your life, such as answering a particular prayer request.

b. Your personal testimony should reveal God as a personal God, help you connect with your interest, and keep the study interesting.

Words to Live By

When we give ourselves wholly to God and in our work follow His directions, He makes Himself responsible for its accomplishment. He would not have us conjecture as to the success of our honest endeavors. Not once should we even think of failure. We are to co-operate with One who knows no failure (*Christ's Object Lessons*, p. 363).

Talents used are talents multiplied. Success is not the result of chance or of destiny; it is the outworking of God's own providence, the reward of faith and discretion, of virtue and persevering effort. The Lord desires us to use every gift we have; and if we do this, we shall have greater gifts to use. He does not supernaturally endow us with the qualifications we lack; but while we use that which we have, He will work with us to increase and strengthen every faculty. By every wholehearted, earnest sacrifice for the Master's service our powers will increase (*Christ's Object Lessons*, p. 353).

Every effort made for Christ will react in blessing upon ourselves. If we use our means for His glory, He will give us more. As we seek to win others to Christ, bearing the burden of souls in our prayers, our own hearts will throb with the quickening influence of God's grace; our own affections will glow with more divine fervor; our whole Christian life will be more of a reality, more earnest, more prayerful (*Christ's Object Lessons*, p. 354).

Weekly Challenge! This week ask a friend, neighbor, or co-worker to begin Bible studies with you! Utilize the canvasses given on Day Four. Imagine how exciting it will be to begin studying the Bible with those whom you love the most! Ask God to reveal to you whose heart is most open to Him; it might not be the person you were expecting! Claim Exodus 4:12—"Now therefore, go, and I will be with your mouth and teach you what you shall say."

Answering the Call, Part Two

From last week's story, Jerrod nearly lost his life while serving as a soldier overseas. After a very painful and tumultuous childhood, he had appreciated the stability of military life. Now with his tour of duty over, all was about to change ...

After two years in enlisted service, Jerrod gladly returned to civilian life. But the scars of his past and the life-threatening encounters in Iraq left him in constant fear. Depression, obesity, and hopelessness sought to smother him once again. Now with three children to feed, failure was not an option.

Though his new degree in human services provided financial stability, he was not satisfied. His heart still yearned for more. Jerrod longed to study God's Word more and share the freedom he had found in Jesus. After hearing of the Amazing Facts Center of Evangelism (AFCOE), Jerrod felt a growing conviction in his heart. Though the financial responsibilities seemed too large, he knew that God was calling him to AFCOE, and this time, he wouldn't look back.

After praying with his wife, Jerrod decided to send three hundred letters to family and friends asking for their support with his AFCOE tuition. But there was a problem—he didn't even have the money to pay the postage! Desperation led him to creativity. Dressed in his "Sunday best," Jerrod stood in front of a local superstore with a sign in hand: "Iraq War Veteran—need help paying for Bible school!" In less than four hours, he had raised all the stamp money that he needed.

As donations continued to pour in, Jerrod packed his car and set off on a sixteen-hour drive—from rural Casper, Wyoming, to the warmth of Albuquerque, New Mexico, for AFCOE's offsite Fall 2014 program. With each passing mile, his anticipation grew as he contemplated the things he would soon learn. He couldn't wait to dive into the book of Revelation, discuss deep theological questions, and practice evangelistic preaching.

Today, however, as he looks back on his AFCOE training, he discovered his greatest joy in an unexpected place—a deeper understanding of the love of Jesus Christ. Jerrod's heart melted as the first two weeks of AFCOE were spent contemplating the life of Christ and His character. As he explored the heart of Jesus, his own heart was transformed. This experience surpassed all his expectations and deepened his passion for the ministry ahead.

With unconstrained excitement, Jerrod stepped out of his car. His heart hadn't raced with excitement like this since his days in Kuwait. The very first day of AFCOE outreach had begun! He quickly moved through his canvass with one middle-aged woman while enjoying a friendly conversation. Though nervous, he finally offered personal in-home Bible studies to her and she accepted! Jerrod was shocked.

Not long into their studies, she revealed that she had been raised as a Seventh-day Adventist. But after being offended by some church members, she had no intention of ever returning. As Jerrod and his outreach partner continued to build a relationship with her and share the promises of God's Word, her heart began to melt. It wasn't long before she became excited to come back "home."

Due to this experience, Jerrod no longer doubted the value of friendship evangelism. Regardless of how many people roam the earth, he recognized that God never forgets His lost lamb crying out for deliverance! He will gladly organize these divine appointments if we are willing to be His hands and feet.

Since AFCOE, Jerrod has begun working as a full-time Bible worker. He has set his hand to the plow. Come what may, by the grace of God, he will not turn back.

Week Eight
*Giving Bible Studies,
Part Two*

FOCUS

"The Lord God has given Me
the tongue of the learned, that
I should know how to speak a
word in season to him who is
weary. He awakens Me morning
by morning, He awakens My
ear to hear as the learned"
(Isaiah 50:4).

INTRODUCTION

A dust cloud billowed in the distance as the rumble of an approaching chariot grew louder. The suffocating heat of the desert intensified for this weary apostle, who was watching from afar. "Why did God bring me away from my work among the multitude to this barren desert?" he may have wondered.

Suddenly, a voice came loud and clear, "Go near and overtake this chariot" (Acts 8:29). Without a second thought, Philip raced ahead with supernatural speed. Over the clamor of the chariot wheels, he heard an Ethiopian voice reading a familiar passage. "Do you understand what you are reading?" Philip inquired.

"How can I, unless someone guides me?", the Ethiopian responded with a sigh of frustration.

Soon Philip was sitting beside this stranger, explaining to him the Words of Life. Through the Messianic prophecy of Isaiah 53, Philip revealed its fulfillment in Jesus Christ, leading to the baptism of the eunuch and the gospel spreading as wildfire throughout the beautiful country of Ethiopia.

From just a simple question, "Do you understand what you're reading?", a door was opened and a man was led to a saving relationship with Christ. Just as Philip did, Jesus also utilized questions effectively in order to create interest and open doors to share the gospel. When a lawyer attempted to trick Him by asking how to have eternal life, Jesus turned the tables and inquired, "What is written in the law? What is your reading of it?" (Luke 10:25, 26). Jesus then told the moving story of the Good Samaritan who had compassion on a dying man—unlike a priest and a Levite—and then asked another question: "Which of these was his neighbor?"

Jesus knew how to pique their curiosity. We all know that "you can lead a horse to water but you can't make it drink." But you can salt its oats! And what happens when you salt a horse's oats? It naturally seeks after the water trough! So also with spiritual things. We can't force someone to be interested in the Bible, but this week we will learn how to pique curiosity and strengthen our Bible study delivery so that many more will desire to drink from that Everlasting Water—and go all the way with Jesus.

THIS WEEK IN THE SCRIPTURES

Prayerfully read these passages before beginning this week's study.

- 1 Corinthians 14:33, 40
- John 18:33–38
- Luke 23:8, 9
- Revelation 3:20
- 1 Corinthians 9:22
- Acts 17:22, 23
- Acts 2:46, 47
- Acts 5:41, 42
- Matthew 5:1–10

Don't Wear Out the Saints

Read — Mark 6:7 and Luke 10:1

React — Jesus sent out the twelve apostles and the seventy disciples two by two. Why is this an important model to follow? What dangers can we face when we go out alone?

_____

_____

_____

Calling the twelve about Him, Jesus bade them go out two and two through the towns and villages. None were sent forth alone, but brother was associated with brother, friend with friend. Thus they could help and encourage each other, counseling and praying together, each one's strength supplementing the other's weakness. In the same manner He afterward sent forth the seventy. It was the Savior's purpose that the messengers of the gospel should be associated in this way. In our own time evangelistic work would be far more successful if this example were more closely followed (*The Desire of Ages*, p. 350).

Your outreach partner should be chosen carefully and prayerfully. Ideally, your partner should be of a different educational background, ethnicity, age group, and experience level. In this way, you will learn from each other and be able to connect with a broader group of Bible study interests.

Your partner may enter into the conversation during social time, but once you start the study, he or she becomes the *silent prayer partner*, playing a vital role as intercessor for you and the interest. If both you and your partner attempt to lead a study together, confusion can often result. The prayer partner should pray for a hedge of angels to protect the study from distractions. He should also pray that the Holy Spirit would reveal truth and speak to the heart, bringing the interest to a decision. Never underestimate the power of a praying partner!

There are two prevalent methods for giving Bible studies: the review method and the presenter method. The review method is when you leave the Bible lesson for your interest to complete on his own and then review it together at a later time. The presenter method is when you bring the Bible lesson with you and present the material. The interest receives the second lesson when you give the second study. You may choose to leave supplementary material to reinforce the material covered during your study.

Keep in mind that when it comes to evangelism, there are a hundred ways to do the right thing. But in this lesson, we recommend utilizing the presenter method, especially when presenting doctrinal studies.

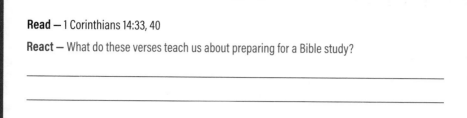

Read — 1 Corinthians 14:33, 40

React — What do these verses teach us about preparing for a Bible study?

_____

_____

_____

Bible studies can be divided into three parts:

Part 1: Social Time — *8 to 10 minutes*

- Spend time getting acquainted and connecting personally.
- Use FORT to start conversations. (See Week 5 – Day 3.)
- Acknowledge things of interest (family pictures on the wall, artwork, etc.).
- Be a good listener.
- Use open body language and eye contact.

Part 2: Body of the Study — *40 to 45 minutes*

- Ask if he has had a chance to work on the lesson.
- Present the Bible study.
- Focus on Christ! Love is the basis of all your lessons because "God is love" (1 John 4:8).
- Ensure that your presentation is relational and personal.

Part 3: Appeal and Decision — *3 to 5 minutes*

- Make an appeal.
- Always ask for a decision.
- Seal the decision in prayer.
- Give the next lesson and leave right away so as not to distract from the Holy Spirit's impressions about what was just learned.

Ellen White humorously emphasized the importance of concise messages by sharing the experiences of others.

"I always know by the length of Cannon's sermon whether he has been much from home during the week," said one of his flock. "When carefully studied, his discourses are of moderate length, but it is almost impossible for his hearers to forget the teachings conveyed in them. When he has had no time for preparation, his sermons are unreasonably long, and it is equally

impossible to get anything out of them which will stick to the memory."
Another able minister was asked how long he was accustomed to preach.
"When I prepare thoroughly, half an hour. When only partially, an hour. But
when I enter the pulpit without previous preparation, I go on for any length of
time you like; in fact I never know when to stop" (*Evangelism*, p. 176).

This is obviously problematic! We never want to wear out our audience.

If we are thoroughly prepared for our Bible studies, we will be able to present
them clearly in a reasonable amount of time. It is best to always keep the study
time less than an hour, though there may be some slight cultural variance.

Even if your Bible study friend wants you to stay longer, it is wise not to take too
much of his time. It is far better for him to be anxious for you to come back than to
dread your visit because you stay so long.

Discuss — List and discuss three benefits gained from keeping your Bible studies concise. What
message does this send to your Bible study friend?

1. _____

   _____

   _____

2. _____

   _____

   _____

3. _____

   _____

   _____

Faithful Fruit Inspectors

Read — John 18:33–38 and Luke 23:8, 9

React — Why did Jesus respond to Pilate's inquiries but not to Herod's? What could this teach us about the difference between ripe fruit and green fruit?

_____

_____

_____

All who show a desire should be given the opportunity to study God's Word. However, we must know and understand the sad reality that not everyone is going to accept the truth. Even the greatest Soul Winner—Jesus—had interests walk away (Mark 10:17–23; John 6:60–66).

We must prayerfully watch for signs to discern the level of interest in our Bible study friends. There will be many who would love to have you come and talk for hours but are not at all interested in spiritual things. If we allow these situations to distract us, we will be leaving the ripe fruit to rot on the trees!

Jesus said, "You will know them by their fruits" (Matthew 7:16). We are never to judge whether people will be saved or lost, but we are to be fruit inspectors and determine which fruit is ripe for harvest. We should spend quality time with those who are ripe for the truth. Those who are green or nearly ripe should still get our attention, but it should be proportionate to their interest level. If we spend the bulk of our time with the green fruit, we could find the ripe fruit passing beyond the point of interest.

Some people are ripe to study. Others are a little green but nearly ripe. Then there are those who haven't even blossomed. How can we identify those who are ripe for Bible studies?

Read — Revelation 3:20 and John 12:32

React — What acts did Christ perform in these scenarios to draw people to Him? Does He ever force His love upon anyone?

_____

_____

_____

Jesus is the perfect Gentleman. He never forces His love; rather, He meekly but persistently knocks at the door. He longs to come in! He yearns to dwell with His people! Yet He will never force Himself on anyone.

So likewise, we must be careful to never force green fruit to accept spiritual things. If we attempt to pick green fruit, it will never taste as good! We must let it ripen on the vine. Remember, if we try to force the Bible on those who are unripe, we could forever destroy their desire for spiritual things.

How then do we know who is ripe and who is not? First, we must pray. Ask God for the knowledge to be "wise as serpents and harmless as doves" (Matthew 10:16). With that prayerful spirit in mind, consider the following characteristics commonly found in ripe and green fruit.

Frequent Characteristics of Ripe Fruit

- Manifest an earnest desire to seek and find Bible truth
- Accept Bible studies and complete the lessons weekly
- Lonely, unhappy, and dissatisfied with their lives
- Feel a need for change
- Dissatisfied with their church
- Don't belong to a church or are backsliding
- Accept major doctrines and make positive decisions
- Display evidence of conviction
- Have shown a change in lifestyle while learning truth
- Desire to share with others what has been learned

These are the types of contacts with whom you want to spend the majority of your time.

Frequent Characteristics of Green Fruit

- Usually will refuse Bible studies
- Often do not have them completed on time
- Make excuses over and over for not completing the study
- Don't accept the clear teachings of Scripture
- Deeply involved in and committed to their own church
- Talk badly about the lesson, your church, or doctrines
- Friendly but won't make any commitments

Discuss — Do we cease all relationships with green fruit? How can we continue to build friendships with them without forcing spiritual things on them? (Hint: Discuss creative ministries!)

_____

_____

_____

Speaking without Words

Read — 1 Corinthians 9:22 and Acts 17:22, 23

React — How did the apostle Paul demonstrate the importance of relating to each person individually?

_____

_____

_____

It is crucial that we, as soul winners, study the human mind and learn how to relate to others, regardless of their backgrounds.

Mechanics, lawyers, merchants, men of all trades and professions, educate themselves that they may become masters of their business. Should the followers of Christ be less intelligent, and while professedly engaged in His service be ignorant of the ways and means to be employed? The enterprise of gaining everlasting life is above every earthly consideration. In order to lead souls to Jesus there must be a knowledge of human nature and a study of the human mind. Much careful thought and fervent prayer are required to know how to approach men and women upon the great subject of truth (_Counsels for the Church_, p. 68).

A huge component of learning how to relate to others is in understanding body language. Are you sitting forward excitedly during your Bible study—or are you leaning back looking rather uninterested? Are you keeping eye contact, especially while the other person is talking—or are you focused on reading your notes? Are you smiling and passionate about what you are sharing—or do you keep stealing glances at your watch? Are you focused on connecting with your study friend and demonstrating how important this study time is—or are you looking at your cell phone?

Evaluate your body language and responses to see how you can improve in the following areas:

- Beware of interrupting or taking a superior position.
- Never demonstrate a lack of interest or having other priorities.
- Be careful of negative reactions or breaking confidence.
- Remember to maintain eye contact without staring.
- Position your body to express interest.

- Ask friendly questions and assume nothing.
- Encourage more sharing.
- Smile; be excited and passionate! If you aren't excited, your study friend won't be either.
- Use your study friend's name frequently.
- Speak clearly. Don't be monotone. Vary your voice according to what you are saying. Don't shout in delicate moments.
- Be a good listener!

Discuss — Choose a partner in your small group. Read Isaiah 61:1–3 as you would to a Bible study friend. After reading the text, give a two- or three-minute explanation—a mini-Bible study. Practice using all of the body language and communication tips mentioned above. Following this practice session, ask your partner what went well and for tips on three areas where you can improve.

_____

_____

_____

Meeting Felt Needs

Read — Acts 2:46, 47 and Acts 5:41, 42

React — What contributed to the unquenchable witnessing power of the early church? What approach did they take in giving Bible studies and what was the result?

_____

_____

_____

The early church exhibited a deep sense of community. They were found daily eating together, fellowshipping, and sharing the Word of God. Because of this close sense of community, many souls were won to a saving relationship with Jesus. We are counseled ...

> Go to your neighbors one by one, and come close to them till their hearts are warmed by your unselfish interest and love. Sympathize with them, pray for them, watch for opportunities to do them good, and as you can, gather a few together and open the Word of God to their darkened minds. Keep watching, as he who must render an account for the souls of men, and make the most of the privileges that God gives you of laboring with Him in His moral vineyard. Do not neglect speaking to your neighbors, and doing them all the kindness in your power, that you "by all means may save some." We need to seek for the spirit that constrained the apostle Paul to go from house to house pleading with tears, and teaching "repentance toward God, and faith toward our Lord Jesus Christ" (*The Review and Herald*, March 13, 1888).

Read — Matthew 10:16; Isaiah 50:4; Matthew 5:1-10

React — How did Jesus demonstrate His ability to minister to the felt needs of others? Is this ability something that comes naturally?

_____

_____

_____

During social time, you are asking questions that will help you discover what some of your study friend's felt needs are. Maybe he is fearful of the final events just before Jesus will come—or of His coming. You would then want to weave into the study some promises that would take away the fear and give comfort, trust, and faith that Jesus will be there and will see us through just as He was there and went through the fire with Daniel's friends. Or maybe he questions his salvation, worrying that he is not good enough or too sinful to ever go to heaven. It could also be a fear of death. Use Bible texts that will address these fears.

Write the promises on cards so he can have them handy when he needs to read them again for assurance. Go through the gospel presentation, leading your friend to Christ. If you sense the need to interrupt your pre-planned lesson and give the gospel presentation instead—do it! This is more important because being weighed down with these concerns can make it difficult to focus on the lesson. Remember that there is power in the Word.

God so loved the world that He gave His only begotten Son, that whoever believes in Him should not perish but have everlasting life (John 3:16).

In every Bible study, use one or two extra texts to supplement your lesson that will deal with your study friend's felt needs and make your study more Christ-centered and love focused. A promise book and a concordance are wonderful reference books for finding these texts.

Discuss — One of the apostle Paul's greatest Bible studies was with King Agrippa (Acts 26). What kind of presentation is a good way to relate to and encourage our Bible study friends when they are having doubts?

_____

_____

_____

Tools You Can Use!

Apply! — Here are eight tips on how to handle difficult situations you may encounter during a Bible study.

1. **If a student is frequently canceling scheduled Bible studies or showing a lack of interest, here are two things you might try saying:**

   "I've noticed that you've had a difficult time finding time to complete these lessons. Are you finding these studies interesting and helpful? If not, I have another set that might be more interesting to you."

   "I am happy to help and encourage you in your Bible study, but I surely don't want you to feel that you have to continue with them. Do you still want to continue the lessons?"

2. **If a student asks a question that is completely unrelated to the subject you're discussing or about a doctrine that would be better presented at a later time, try saying one of the following:**

   "That's a very good question! We are going to have a whole lesson on that subject a little later on. If you don't mind, can we discuss it more thoroughly at that time?"

   You might tell him that you would like him to find the answer to the question by researching what the Bible has to say. Show him how to use a concordance and give the key words to look up. (For example, if the question is about baptism, have him look up all the New Testament texts with the words "buried," "baptize," and "water.") Have him write the texts down and ask himself, "What does this text say about this subject?" Then have him write this point down. After assembling all these key points, he should have a good idea about the answer to the question. Have him share with you next time. This is an excellent way to help people find answers.

3. **If a student asks you a question for which you don't know the answer, say:**

   "That's a good question. But, to tell you the truth, I've not thought about that question before. I will study it out this week and share what I've learned next week."

   "That's a good question. I'm not sure what the Bible says about it. What have you found or heard?"

4. **If a student brings up an observation that you aren't familiar with or an argument against truth that you don't know the Bible's answer to:**

Realize that it isn't necessary for you to have something to say in response to every thought a person shares. This is true even if it is something you know to be erroneous. It might be best to just nod your head and say, "That's an interesting point."

If the thought is one that you must answer because it means the difference between the person obeying truth or not, you can say, "I can see that you have a serious question you want answered before you go any further on this topic. Would you like for me to prepare some material for your research on this topic for our next study?"

If he is repeating what someone else told him, don't necessarily think that you have to defend the truth. Be quiet and listen to what he has to say. Ask him what he thinks about the person's comments. You will often find that he will answer his own question, showing that he has already thought it through and defended the truth.

5. **If children interrupt the study:**

Suggest a time to study when the children would be in bed, taking a nap, or at school.

Bring someone with you to give a children's program/Bible study while you study with the adults.

Take a coloring book or a well-illustrated storybook for the children.

6. **The TV is left on during your study:**

Ask, "Is this your favorite program?" or "Would it be okay to turn down the television while we study?" In both instances, they will then realize that the TV is on and will typically just turn it off.

7. **A neighbor is at the house when you arrive, or arrives during your study:**

After graciously meeting the neighbor, invite him to join your study. Explain what you are doing and briefly review what you've discussed.

If the subject is a delicate or controversial one, say, "I'm sorry but I haven't had the chance to give you the necessary background for the study we are doing. May I spend some time with you later to help you get the background you need? I think it will mean a lot more to you. I don't like anyone to go away confused about the Bible because of things I've shared."

If absolutely necessary, you might ask your study friend, "Would you like to continue with the study now or would it be better for me to come back later?"

8. **The student says, "I just can't see this," or, "I can't agree with this," or, "This is certainly different than what I believe."**

"You know, I came up against the same thing myself. I had to say to myself, 'This is certainly different from what I've believed, but if it is what the Bible teaches, and if it is what Jesus said, then it is what I want.' "

"As we endeavor to find the Lord's will, I think the most important test for any teaching is, 'Is this what the Bible really teaches? Is there a 'thus says the Lord' here?"

"Is there any way I can help by clarifying what we have studied?"

"I understand that this subject may be new and different to you. May I leave these texts with you to consider?" Or, "May I share a pamphlet with you on this subject that you might find helpful?"

Words to Live By

You must come close to those for whom you labor, that they may not only hear your voice, but shake your hand, learn your principles, feel your sympathy (*Gospel Workers,* p. 192).

Many a laborer fails in his work because he does not come close to those who most need his help (*Gospel Workers,* p. 190).

The Lord desires that His word of grace shall be brought home to every soul. To a great degree this must be accomplished by personal labor. This was Christ's method. His work was largely made up of personal interviews. He had a faithful regard for the one-soul audience. Through that one soul the message was often extended to thousands. We are not to wait for souls to come to us; we must seek them out where they are. When the word has been preached in the pulpit, the work has but just begun. There are multitudes who will never be reached by the gospel unless it is carried to them (*Christ's Object Lessons,* p. 229).

Weekly Challenge! If you haven't already, now is the time to ask two family members, friends, neighbors, or co-workers to begin Bible studies with you! If you are currently giving a Bible study, review the material presented in this lesson, and choose three principles that you want to specifically utilize and strengthen during your Bible study this week. Be sure to practice your study on a friend from your small group and ask for advice on how you can improve.

The Tattooed Prayer Warrior

A story from Jëan Ross, V.P. of Evangelism

"C'mon, Pat! Just come three times and I promise I'll never bother you again," his brother pled. Pat was not an easy person to persuade. His shaved head and tattooed arms were a fearsome sight to most. Known in town for his popular tattoo parlor and gang activities, no one crossed Pat's path; but Rob was not afraid. He knew this might be his last chance to bring his brother to a decision for Christ.

After much coaxing and a promise to never discuss religious things again if he came, Pat grudgingly agreed to attend a local prophecy seminar. The battle, however, was far from won.

On opening night, Rob drove by Pat's house to pick him up for the evening meeting. "I'm not going," Pat growled.

"But Pat—you promised!" his brother gently coaxed. With many a complaint and frustrated sighs, Pat finally plopped himself into the passenger seat as he rode to church for the first time in decades.

At the venue, every head turned in utter shock. "The infamous drug dealer? Gangster? Tattoo artist? At our church?" The questions were written across every face. Yet in typical Pat style, he noisily sat down with a sigh of annoyance. During the entire message that night, Pat made every commotion possible, attempting to demonstrate just how much he hated every minute of this torture. "I'm never coming back here again!" he huffed—the words bringing a near sigh of relief from listening church members.

"You promised!" Rob replied. He was not ready to give up on his lost and confused brother.

The second night was no better. Again, Pat loudly sighed and fidgeted throughout the entirety of the seminar, bringing yet again a sigh of relief from the church as he walked out the door. But on the third night, something unexpected occurred. Something that would change his future forever ...

Without even realizing it, Pat caught himself actually listening. He leaned forward in his chair, trying to catch the pastor's every word. *"You mean Jesus could still love someone like me?"* His heart longed for an answer. Suddenly his chair began to shake violently as Pat's shoulders heaved in heartfelt sobs. When the appeal was given, Pat could not hold back. At the front of a church, with all eyes glued upon him, Pat gave his life and heart to his Savior, Jesus Christ.

Pat became an instant soul winner for Christ. He excitedly shared all that he had learned and encouraged others to meet Jesus for themselves. It wasn't long before he and his girlfriend were married and then baptized, to the great joy of his faithful brother.

An opportunity soon presented itself for Pat's testimony to be shared far beyond small-town America where he was raised. He never dreamed he'd be standing in the beautiful country of India, watching the swirl of activity around him and smelling the fragrant spices of the Far East. Each night he faithfully assisted the prophecy seminar speaker, Jëan Ross, in managing the audio equipment and assisting with logistics. But one night, Pat disappeared.

Jëan scanned the crowds, hoping to spot this faithful friend. Suddenly, he saw him—way off in the distance. There Pat stood, surrounded by a group of Indian women, his hands placed customarily upon their heads in prayer. The very hands that once brought fear to all within reach were now gently placed on heads in prayer as Pat sought the God of heaven on their behalf.

With a smile spread across his face and joy filling his heart, Jëan exclaimed, "There truly is a God in heaven who changes lives." That same God longs to change our lives and the lives of our family and friends!

Week Nine
Answering Objections

FOCUS

"If any of you lacks wisdom, let him ask of God, who gives to all liberally and without reproach, and it will be given to him" (James 1:5).

INTRODUCTION

With brows furrowed in anger, the religious leaders listened attentively. Of all people, surely this lawyer would aid their cause by trapping Jesus in an endless argument.

"Teacher, what shall I do to inherit eternal life?" (Luke 10:25). This question, though asked with sincerity, brought an unexpected answer and deep conviction to his heart. Seeking to justify himself, he continued, "And who is my neighbor?" (verse 29).

> Among the Jews this question caused endless dispute. They had no doubt as to the heathen and the Samaritans; these were strangers and enemies. But where should the distinction be made among the people of their own nation, and among the different classes of society? Whom should the priest, the rabbi, the elder, regard as neighbor? They spent their lives in a round of ceremonies to make themselves pure. Contact with the ignorant and careless multitude, they taught, would cause defilement that would require wearisome effort to remove. Were they to regard the "unclean" as neighbors? Again Jesus refused to be drawn into controversy. He did not denounce the bigotry of those who were watching to condemn Him. But by a simple story He held up before His hearers such a picture of the outflowing of heaven-born love as touched all hearts, and drew from the lawyer a confession of the truth (*The Desire of Ages*, p. 498).

Christ's approach in dealing with arguments can be applied effectively still today! We are counseled, "The way to dispel darkness is to admit light. The best way to deal with error is to present truth. It is the revelation of God's love that makes manifest the deformity and sin of the heart centered in self" (ibid.).

An objection is an obstacle people face as they encounter ideas contrary to their own way of thinking. Jesus was a master at answering objections. When

Lucifer tempted Him in the wilderness regarding obedience to God, three times Jesus gave the wise answer, "It is written." Jesus used Scripture to deflect the fiery darts that were thrown at Him by Satan. In the same way, all successful soul winners must know how to deal with objections using a kind, Christ-centered approach. Remember, very few people make up their minds to accept truth and unite with God's last-day church without a struggle.

If there is one thing that new Bible instructors fear more than anything else, it is objections. Often we look at objections as barriers, when we should view them as opportunities to lead precious souls to Jesus and His truth.

This week we will consider effective ways of responding to objections, while lifting up Jesus and reaching the heart.

THIS WEEK IN THE SCRIPTURES
Prayerfully read these passages before beginning this week's study.

- 2 Timothy 2:23–25
- John 11:30–35
- Romans 12:15, 16
- John 4:19–24
- Mark 13:11
- Acts 17:16–28

Reaching the Heart

Read — 2 Timothy 2:23-25; Colossians 4:6; James 1:19, 20

React — How should a Christian respond to arguments? Why is it that we have a tendency to become defensive or irritated when challenged with questions?

_____

_____

_____

Regardless of how rudely a question is phrased or how argumentative a person may be, a Christian is never to enter this battlefield. Rather, seek ways to apply Christ's method of disarming His opponents and meeting the true heart needs beneath the angry façade. Always—always!—respond in love and kindness.

It is important for our Bible study friends to feel affirmed in their dialogue with us. Consider using positive phrases such as: "That's a very good question." "I'm glad you expressed your concerns." Intentionally affirming in a kind and calm way results in frustrations quickly simmering down.

Read — Isaiah 63:9 and John 11:30-35

React — How does Christ respond to our suffering? How did He respond to the suffering He witnessed around the tomb of Lazarus? What does this teach us about how we are to respond to others?

_____

_____

_____

Jesus knew that Lazarus would soon rise from the dead. He knew that soon all sorrow would be vanquished by joy! Why then did Jesus weep?

At least two reasons are recorded in the book _The Desire of Ages_. For one, Jesus wept for those standing there who would never accept the eternal life found in Him and would soon enter their own sealed tomb. But more so, "Though He was the Son of God, yet He had taken human nature upon Him, and He was moved by human sorrow. His tender, pitying heart is ever awakened to sympathy by suffering. He weeps with those that weep, and rejoices with those that rejoice" (p. 533).

Jesus cannot remain aloof from human suffering. He sees past the anger, past the accusing questions, and sees the pain of the human heart. We must learn to look beyond cold exteriors and truly reach the heart.

Discuss — *Gospel Workers*, p. 193, reminds us, "Your success will not depend so much upon your knowledge and accomplishments, as upon your ability to find your way to the heart." How can we find the way to the heart? How can we apply Christ's method of peeling back the layers in order to meet the true needs within?

_____

_____

_____

Can You Hear Me Now?

Read — Proverbs 18:13 and Isaiah 30:21

React — What do these verses teach us about the importance of listening carefully to others and to God? Why do we often find it so difficult to listen attentively?

_____

_____

_____

Before you try to diagnose the problem, allow your Bible study friends to fully explain their questions or concerns. (Remember that God gave us two ears but only one mouth!) Your goal while you listen to the objection is to discover what really hinders them from making a positive decision. You could give Bible studies endlessly with little to no progress if you don't first discover what their true objections are.

While listening to your study friends, maintain eye contact and body language that lets them know you're listening and that you care. Never interrupt or argue and always maintain a soft tone in your voice. Otherwise, you could win the argument but lose a friend. Always dwell on the affirmative and not the negative points.

Often, as you seek to present the truth, opposition will be aroused; but if you seek to meet the opposition with argument you will only multiply it, and that you cannot afford to do. Hold to the affirmative. Angels of God are watching you, and they understand how to impress those whose opposition you refuse to meet with argument (_Testimonies for the Church_, Vol. 9, p. 147).

The goal is to instill a feeling of confidence in your friends that they can come to you with real questions and real concerns. Always encourage them to express their ideas, even if their ideas may seem preposterous.

Read — 1 Peter 3:8; Romans 12:15, 16; Matthew 9:35, 36; Hebrews 4:15

React — What do these verses have in common? How can we genuinely experience this heart of compassion in our own lives—not just for our friends, but for those who have hurt us or treated us poorly?

_____

_____

_____

With eager expectation, the excited crowd began to move through town. Suddenly their smiles faded and their happy chatter stopped as the heart wrenching cries of a devastated mother pierced the air. He was the widow's only son: her joy, her confidant, and her provider. Her heart was broken to the core.

Jesus, upon the sight of this grief-stricken woman, was moved with compassion. His heart yearned to comfort her as He gently begged, "Do not weep," before touching the open coffin and raising her beloved son back from the dead.

The heart of Christ cannot remain unmoved at the sight of suffering humanity. Just as Christ empathized with those who craved it most, we too are called to meet the heart needs of all around us.

One of the most effective ways to handle objections and reach the heart is to use the three Fs: **F**eel, **F**elt, **F**ound. Use the three Fs frequently when objections begin to surface.

Feel — "I understand the way you feel."
As you demonstrate your interest, love, and acceptance to your friends, you will win their confidence.

Felt — "Many others in your situation have felt exactly the same way."
No one likes to feel all alone in a situation. Share a story of someone you know who went through a similar experience.

Found — "But they have found ..."
The answer is always found in Jesus! Did they find that God answers prayers? That God's plan was so much better than theirs? How did they find security in Christ?

Discuss — In your small group, discuss two situations in which the three Fs would be beneficial. Consider examples such as a single mom who might lose her job if she keeps the Sabbath—or a man who is angry that God allowed his wife to die from cancer. Role-play these scenarios with your small group and attempt to use them this week with your friends or co-workers as the need arises.

Humble Reliance

Read — John 4:19-24

React — When under conviction, the Samaritan woman quickly shifted the discussion away from herself to religious and political arguments. How did Jesus respond to this distraction? What lessons can we learn from His approach?

_____

_____

_____

Conviction was poking at her heart. Who was this man? How did He know her life story? She quickly changed topics, hoping to ease her mind and prevent any more vulnerability. But Jesus didn't bite on her attempted distraction. He would enter into no political or cultural debate. "God is Spirit, and those who worship Him must worship in spirit and truth" (John 4:24), He calmly replied.

Jesus was never caught off guard by arguments. His mind was fastened on the Father as He sought to find an avenue to the heart. We too must understand that we don't have all of the answers, but God does! He will provide the words when we need them most.

Read — 2 Timothy 2:15; James 1:5; Mark 13:11

React — How do we reconcile these verses? Is there a balance between being prepared for future objections through the study of God's Word and in simply trusting (or presuming?) that He'll provide the answers without us studying for ourselves?

_____

_____

_____

The Holy Spirit will bring back to remembrance only those things that we have studied. We must continue to "grow in the grace and knowledge of our Lord" (2 Peter 3:18), while relying on His wisdom to prepare us for the work ahead. "If the worker keeps his heart uplifted in prayer, God will help him to speak the right word at the right time" (_Gospel Workers_, p. 120).

Below are some responses that can be used effectively to answer difficult questions during your study:

"I'm glad you have shared this with me. I can see that this means a lot to you, and I believe that the Lord has the answer. Let's search God's Word together."

"That's a great question! We are going to have a whole lesson on that very subject in just a couple weeks. If you don't mind, can we discuss it more thoroughly at that time?"

It is important to let your study friends know that you can find the answer together. This puts you in a new light; it is not you on the one side and them on the other. You are now on their side; you're a team! Show them how to use a concordance and give them key words to look up.

Discuss — Is it OK to tell your study friend that you don't know the answer? What are the positive or negative results of doing so? Why is it so important for your study friends to see that you too are a humble student seeking to understand God's Word?

_____

_____

_____

Adventism's Four Cs

Read — Acts 17:16-28

React — Why did the apostle Paul use this approach of sharing Christ through the altar of the "unknown God"? Why did he not begin his discourse by simply confronting their error and idolatry?

_____

_____

_____

Paul sought an avenue to every heart. He used that which was of greatest interest and value to them in order to start a spiritual conversation. He did not enter the arena with fists flying; rather, he looked for ways in which they could relate.

Have you ever been asked, "You're a Seventh-day Adventist? What do you believe?" How often we quickly reply by listing all twenty-eight of our fundamental beliefs. By the end of our discourse, they are often left feeling confused and distant.

It would be wise to consider these counsels ...

In laboring in a new field, do not think it your duty to say at once to the people, We are Seventh-day Adventists; we believe that the seventh day is the Sabbath; we believe in the nonimmortality of the soul. This would often erect a formidable barrier between you and those you wish to reach (_Evangelism_, p. 200).

Every advantage should be taken to get acquainted with these men; not in a way to produce anything like prejudice. We must appear to them as trying to help others, working on the line of the Christian help work. As they see the good work we do on these lines, their prejudice will be removed in a large measure, and their hearts will be open for more. Then we should not present the Sabbath, but let us present Christ. What if they should begin to oppose you and say, Oh, that's a Seventh-day Adventist?—Lift Christ up higher and still higher. It means a great deal to be wise as serpents and harmless as doves (_Manuscript Releases_, Vol. 5, p. 67).

How then should we respond when confronted with a potentially divisive challenge about Adventists? One of the most effective and unifying responses is Adventism's Four Cs:

1. **CHRIST** — Jesus is the divine Son of God. He is God in the form of a human. He is eternal and self-existent and is _not_ a created being. He is fully God and man. Jesus is the Creator of all things. _Hebrews 1:1-3; Colossians 1:16-18._

2. **CROSS** — Jesus paid the penalty for man's sin through His suffering and death on the cross of Calvary. Only He, the Sinless One, could pay our sin-debt. "The wages of sin is death," but by believing on Him and accepting the grace of His shed blood, we receive the gift of eternal life, "not of works, lest any man should boast." *Romans 6:23; 2 Corinthians 5:19; Ephesians 2:9.*

3. **COMMANDMENTS** — Because we love Jesus for His sacrificial death, we want to obey Him as He commands us in John 14:15. We are not saved by our works. But because of our saving relationship with Christ, we choose to keep His commandments as the guide for successful living.

4. **COMING AGAIN** — One of the greatest promises in the Bible is that Jesus will return to this earth very soon! Bible prophecy reveals that very fact based on the events we see happening in our world today. We call ourselves Adventists because we are anticipating the "advent," or return, of Jesus when He will take His people back to heaven with Him.

Is this not a beautiful picture of Adventism? Use these exciting tools to make eternal friendships for Christ today!

Discuss — Read 1 Corinthians 2:2; John 17:3; and 1 John 5:12. Who is at the core of our belief system? Why is it so crucial to emphasize this throughout our Bible studies with seeking friends?

_____

_____

_____

Tools You Can Use!

Below are five extra tips you can use to be a more effective listener and powerful soul winner for Christ!

1. **Show your Bible study friends that you understand their objections by repeating them in your own words.**

   "Do I understand that the issue holding you back is opposition that you may receive from your _____?"

   "Do I have it correctly that what is really concerning you is _____?"

2. **Learn to separate genuine questions from common excuses.** You can do this by asking specific questions.

   "Is this the only thing holding you back?"

   "If this obstacle were removed, would you then see your way clear to _____ (keep the Sabbath, be baptized, etc.)?" The goal here should be to get a commitment that if the objections were cleared up, then your study friends would make a decision right away.

3. **Answer their questions from the Bible.** When responding to an objection, you want your answer to be concise. An effective way of accomplishing this is by using a Bible text as the basis for all your answers. A good example of what to say would be:

   "I am so glad you asked about the Sabbath. Let's turn to the Word of God and see what it has to say."

   People will argue over personal opinions, but will generally be more open to the words of Scripture. After you give your answer, ask if it cleared up the question. If so, you can move on to the next task; if not, spend more time clarifying what you said by sharing more Bible promises.

4. **Ask them questions.** Christ often responded to a question by asking another question, encouraging seekers to reflect upon the answer for themselves. This also ensures that we have heard their concern correctly. For instance, after learning about the seventh-day Sabbath, Bible study friends will often say, "I spoke with my pastor and he said that it doesn't matter which day we keep." Before turning to Scripture, ask your friends:

   "What did you think about his statement?"

   "How did you respond to him?"

   You might just find that they didn't actually agree with him after all!

5. **If you are not able to clear up an objection when it is first asked, always leave the door open for a follow-up study.** End the visit by saying:

"Before I go, can I have a prayer with you that the Lord will help us with answering this question and give us wisdom to do the right thing?" You can also share about the noble Bereans in Acts 17:10, 11, and encourage them to join you in seeking to be a Berean by searching the Scriptures daily and following what God reveals.

Words to Live By

If the worker keeps his heart uplifted in prayer, God will help him to speak the right word at the right time (*Gospel Workers*, p. 120).

Hot heads and cold hearts never solved anything (Billy Graham).

Often, as you seek to present the truth, opposition will be aroused; but if you seek to meet the opposition with argument, you will only multiply it, and this you cannot afford to do. Hold to the affirmative. Angels of God are watching you, and they understand how to impress those whose opposition you refuse to meet with arguments. Dwell not on the negative points of questions that arise, but gather to your minds affirmative truths, and fasten them there by much study, earnest prayer, and heart consecration. Keep your lamps trimmed and burning, and let bright rays shine forth, that men, beholding your good works, may be led to glorify your Father who is in heaven (*Evangelism*, p. 302).

Weekly Challenge! Is there a relationship between you and someone in your family or church family that needs to be reconciled? God truly is in the midst of reconciliation and yearns to have His children united! (See Matthew 18:15, 19, 20). Prayerfully consider how you can use the 3 Fs or the 4 Cs to bring about witnessing opportunities or reconciliation this week! Share the results with your small group next week.

Out of the Mouth of Babes

A story from Pastor Doug Batchelor

His father was one of the biggest drug dealers in Hawaii, and his mother was a professional shoplifter. Using distraction, she could push a shopping cart full of merchandise out of the store undetected. Perhaps that's why they gave their youngest son the name Diamond. With their parents often away from home for days, Diamond and his four older siblings grew accustomed to fending for themselves. Despite his unstable home life, Diamond learned to read and write and had a voracious hunger for history.

One day, while digging through a box of cookbooks at his grandmother's house, he found a well-worn book called *The Great Controversy*. Even though he was only eleven years old, Diamond read the entire six-hundred-page classic on the battle between good and evil and the history of the Christian church. He knew this book contained truth. For the first time, he knew that there truly was a purpose for life. But he hungered for more!

Diamond asked his grandmother where she got this fascinating book. In response, the next Sabbath morning she dropped him off at a local Adventist church. The members saw how eager the inquisitive visitor was to study, so someone gave the young man a copy of the Amazing Facts *Prophecy Code* seminar series. Soon after completing the DVD set, he surrendered his life to the Lord and was baptized. Diamond continued to read, watch, and listen to all the Amazing Facts material he could find in print, on TV and radio, and online.

Incredibly, at only twelve years of age, Diamond felt God was calling him to ministry, so he enrolled himself in the local Christian school and paid his own tuition by selling Christian books, along with the Amazing Facts *Final Events* DVDs and *Hidden Truth* magazines.

Three years later, Diamond became involved in teaching and preaching. At seventeen, he baptized his other grandmother, a former Baptist, after sharing the messages of truth with her. Upon graduating from high school, Diamond was immediately asked to pastor a local congregation and began to travel to other islands doing revival meetings and evangelism.

Now, as a nineteen-year-old wise beyond his years, Diamond is traveling across North America and around the world preaching the three angels' messages and leading others to Christ.

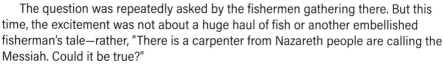

Week Ten
Gaining Decisions for Christ

FOCUS

"If it seems evil to you to serve the LORD, choose for yourselves this day whom you will serve. ... But as for me and my house, we will serve the LORD" (Joshua 24:15).

INTRODUCTION

The shores were buzzing with excitement.

"Have you heard?"

The question was repeatedly asked by the fishermen gathering there. But this time, the excitement was not about a huge haul of fish or another embellished fisherman's tale—rather, "There is a carpenter from Nazareth people are calling the Messiah. Could it be true?"

Peter and Andrew couldn't help but sense the excitement as they went about their work, casting their large net into the calm sea. James and John were also distracted as they attempted to mend their nets without missing a word from the conversations swirling around them. "A healer? A teacher? The Christ?" the thoughts raced through their minds.

Suddenly the carpenter was seen, walking calmly but determinedly along the shore of Galilee—the very one who had filled their conversations just moments before. As He approached them, they heard these life-changing words: "Follow Me, and I will make you fishers of men" (Matthew 4:19). Without a moment of hesitation, they rose from their nets, from their profitable careers and sustenance, and followed a new life course in the footsteps of Jesus Christ.

Jesus was not afraid to call people to make decisions. He did not fear rejection. As He saw the Spirit leading, He beckoned others to follow.

On the contrary, for most people involved in evangelism, we fear rejection and it is our greatest handicap. We may be comfortable giving a Bible study, but when we reach the point of asking our study friends to make a decision, our palms go sweaty and our hearts begin to race.

How do you lead others to make a decision for Jesus Christ? How do you structure your appeal? How would you respond if they say no? This week we aim to take the fear out of asking for decisions by studying the four Cs of gaining decisions—captivate, convince, convict, convert. This simple tool can take away the apprehension and replace it with excitement as you see your friends making positive decisions for Christ!

THIS WEEK IN THE SCRIPTURES
Prayerfully read these passages before beginning this week's study.

- John 3:1–14
- Matthew 7:24–27
- Matthew 21:28–32
- Luke 16:19–31
- John 16:7–13
- Proverbs 4:18
- Acts 16:25–34

Captivate

Read — John 3:1–14

React — How did Jesus captivate the attention of Nicodemus? In what other Bible stories did Jesus use a similar approach?

_____

_____

_____

Jesus knew how to catch the attention of His audience. He often accomplished this by asking questions or making statements that seemed contrary to all they had ever known.

Here's another instance when Jesus captured the interest of His audience:

As Jesus spoke in the temple court, the people were held spellbound. The very men who were the most violent against Him felt themselves powerless to do Him harm. For the time, all other interests were forgotten. Day after day He taught the people, until the last, "that great day of the feast." The morning of this day found the people wearied from the long season of festivity. Suddenly Jesus lifted up His voice, in tones that rang through the courts of the temple: "If any man thirst, let him come unto Me, and drink. He that believeth on Me, as the scripture hath said, out of his belly shall flow rivers of living water." The condition of the people made this appeal very forcible. They had been engaged in a continued scene of pomp and festivity, their eyes had been dazzled with light and color, and their ears regaled with the richest music; but there had been nothing in all this round of ceremonies to meet the wants of the spirit, nothing to satisfy the thirst of the soul for that which perishes not. Jesus invited them to come and drink of the fountain of life, of that which would be in them a well of water, springing up unto everlasting life (*The Desire of Ages*, p. 453).

Read — Matthew 7:24–27; Matthew 21:28–31; Luke 16:19–31

React — What other approaches did Jesus use to capture the attention of the curious crowd around him?

_____

_____

_____

We're told, "Jesus sought an avenue to every heart. By using a variety of illustrations, He not only presented truth in its different phases, but appealed to the different hearers. Their interest was aroused by figures drawn from the surroundings of their daily life. None who listened to [Him] could feel that they were neglected or forgotten. The humblest, the most sinful, heard in His teaching a voice that spoke to them in sympathy and tenderness" (*Christ's Object Lessons*, p. 21).

Discuss — There are three primary types of learners—auditory, visual, and kinesthetic. In order to captivate, approach each learner in a different way with the same story—for example, the second coming of Christ.

- For the kinesthetic learner, use phrases such as "*feel* the warmth of Christ's embrace."
- For the visual learner, you should consider saying, "You will *see* the joy in Jesus' face as He looks upon you with approval."
- For the auditory learner, emphasize "the loud blast of the trumpet" and "the voice of an archangel ringing throughout the heavens."

Practice — Create an appeal for baptism using 2 Corinthians 5:17 as your basis. In your appeal, use words that auditory, visual, and kinesthetic learners could relate to.

_____

_____

_____

Convince

Read — Acts 17:10, 11; 1 Thessalonians 5:21; Isaiah 28:10

React — What principles do these texts teach us about how to grow in our knowledge and relationship with God?

_____

_____

_____

Eternal life comes from knowing Jesus (John 17:3). This knowledge takes time. Relationships are not formed overnight; they must grow in intimacy as communication deepens and commitments are formed.

Imagine a woman on a blind date. For the first time, she's meeting the young man—on her very first date, eating pasta, and staring into the candlelight. The man gazes adoringly into her eyes and inquires, "Will you marry me?"

"Absolutely not!" she retorts.

"But why not?"

Because, "I don't *know* you!"

The woman doesn't have enough information to enter into a trust relationship with this individual. Don't you agree that she'd be rather irrational to commit to a long-term relationship with a person she just met?

This illustration applies as we seek to call people to make decisions for Christ. Before they can make a decision, they must have adequate information. They must see this information clearly from the Bible, and not from our own opinions. If we call for a decision before there is adequate information, as in the blind date example, individuals will almost always make a negative decision. And once a negative decision is made, it will be very difficult to pull down that wall. Ensure that your Bible study friends have adequate information to make an informed decision, one based solely upon the Word of God.

Read — John 16:12 and Proverbs 4:18

React — What do these verses mean? What do they teach us about the importance of revealing truth gradually?

_____

_____

_____

Imagine if you were to build a house with strong walls and a sturdy roof without first laying a firm foundation. What would happen? A deadly collapse! The same is true in evangelism.

Nothing scares an evangelist more than hearing a guest excitedly report toward the end of the series, "I can't wait to go to all my Catholic relatives and reveal who the antichrist really is!" The evangelist will quickly remind him that there is a reason why this topic is not presented on the first night of the prophecy seminar—it would be overwhelming! Truth must be revealed gradually.

Jesus recognized this principle. Though He longed to reveal everything to the disciples, He knew He had to hold back as they were not ready to receive it yet (see also Matthew 16:20, 21 and Mark 9:9). We must remember that the path of the just *grows* brighter and brighter; to shine truth full force with all we have learned through the years would merely blind a new believer.

Discuss — Read the following quotes and ask what three lessons we can draw from this counsel:

I have been shown that our ministers go too rapidly through their subjects and bring the most objectionable features of our faith too early into their effort. There are truths that will not involve so great a cross, that should be kept before their minds, day after day and even weeks before the Sabbath and immortality questions are entered upon. Then you gain the confidence of the people as being men who have clear, forcible arguments, and they think you understand the Scriptures. When once the confidence of the people is gained, then it is time enough to introduce publicly the Sabbath and immortality questions (*Evangelism*, p. 246).

Every advantage should be taken to get acquainted with these men; not in a way to produce anything like prejudice. We must appear to them as trying to help others, working on the line of the Christian help work. As they see the good work we do on these lines, their prejudice will be removed in a large measure, and their hearts will be open for more. Then we should not present the Sabbath, but let us present Christ. What if they should begin to oppose you and say, Oh, that's a Seventh-day Adventist?—Lift Christ up higher and still higher. It means a great deal to be wise as serpents and harmless as doves (*Manuscript Releases,* Vol. 5, p. 67).

1. _____

   _____

2. _____

   _____

3. _____

   _____

Convict

Read — John 16:7, 8, 13

React — According to this passage, what is the role of the Holy Spirit? Do we sometimes try to be the voice of the Holy Spirit to others? Why do we do this? Is it ever successful?

_____

_____

_____

 In John 14:16–18, Jesus promised His beloved followers that He would not leave them as orphans but would send the Holy Spirit as a Comforter to them. In John 16:8, Jesus defined the Holy Spirit's role: "When He has come, He will convict the world of sin, and of righteousness, and of judgment." The word convict means "to "bring to the light, to expose." We don't often think of conviction as being very comforting, but when it is brought by the Holy Spirit, His clear guidance and assuring presence speaks to our hearts as no other voice can.

 If the Holy Spirit is the one bringing conviction, what then is our role during this time? We must pray! Pray for the powers of darkness to be removed and for the Holy Spirit to continue working powerfully in our lives and in the lives of others.

 In Luke 22:31, 32, we read, "The Lord said, 'Simon, Simon! Indeed, Satan has asked for you, that he may sift you as wheat. But I have prayed for you, that your faith should not fail; and when you have returned to Me, strengthen your brethren.' " You see, even in the time of His greatest agony, Jesus recognized the power of intercessory prayer. This begs the question: "Why do not believers feel a deeper, more earnest concern for those who are out of Christ? Why do not two or three meet together and plead with God for the salvation of some special one, and then for still another?" (*Testimonies for the Church*, Vol. 7, p. 21).

Read — Acts 7:59–8:3

React — How did Saul respond after witnessing the martyrdom of Stephen? Would any conviction he might have experienced immediately have led to baptism?

_____

_____

_____

 His blood boiled deep within him. As conviction lay on his heart, Saul must have thought, "If only these Christians were destroyed, then I could have peace!" This conviction, rather than leading to immediate conversion, led a vengeful Saul to seek the murder of more Christian men and women.

Saul's story offers crucial insight for us today. How often do we see only anger when God sees a convicted heart? We may think that individuals are completely uninterested and beyond the reach of God, when in fact their frustration could be a sign that the Holy Spirit is already pursuing their heart. Instead of working against the Spirit, see this anger as a call to more fervent prayer on their behalf!

Read — From *Evangelism*, p. 283:

> It is the work of the Holy Spirit to convince the soul of its need of Christ. Many are convicted of sin, and feel their need of a sin-pardoning Saviour; but they are merely dissatisfied with their pursuits and aims, and if there is not a decided application of the truth to their hearts, if words are not spoken at the right moment, calling for decision from the weight of evidence already presented, the convicted ones pass on without identifying themselves with Christ, the golden opportunity passes, and they have not yielded, and they go farther and farther away from the truth, farther away from Jesus and never take their stand on the Lord's side.

Discuss — According to this passage, what is the danger of postponing an appeal to accept Christ? How can we learn to work in partnership with the Holy Spirit, without running ahead of Him?

_____

_____

_____

Convert

Read — Acts 16:25–34

React — After seeing the example of these Spirit-filled apostles and hearing the beautiful gospel, the prison keeper was captivated, convinced, and convicted. What did this conviction lead him to do? How did he demonstrate his conversion?

_____

_____

_____

"Every man and woman who is truly converted will be a diligent worker" (*Christ's Object Lessons,* p. 343). True conversion leads to action. These two elements should not be separated. As in the life of the jailer, as we experience conversion, it leads to a transformation in every area of our lives. But thank the Lord that He is the one doing the work! (Philippians 2:13). We simply must be open to His voice and be willing to move forward with Him as the Spirit transforms our lives.

Read — Joshua 24:15 and John 12:35, 36

React — *What do these verses teach us about the importance of not delaying decisions for Christ? How do we share these verses without becoming pushy?*

_____

_____

_____

We're told: "There are souls in every congregation who are hesitating, almost persuaded to be wholly for God. The decision is being made for time and for eternity; but it is too often the case that the minister has not the spirit and power of the message of truth in his own heart, hence no direct appeals are made to those souls that are trembling in the balance. The result is that impressions are not deepened upon the hearts of the convicted ones; and they leave the meeting feeling less inclined to accept the service of Christ than when they came. They decide to wait for a more favorable opportunity; but it never comes" (*Testimonies for the Church,* Vol. 4, p. 446).

What a crucial calling we have to lead others to make a decision for Christ at the end of every single Bible study!

Discuss — "Some may be listening to the last sermon they will ever hear, and some will never again be so situated that they can have the chain of truth brought before them and a practical application made of it to their hearts. That golden opportunity lost is lost forever. Had Christ and His redeeming love been exalted in connection with the theory of truth, it might have balanced them on His side" (*Testimonies for the Church*, Vol. 4, p. 393).

What are three lessons we can draw from this warning?

1. _____

_____

2. _____

_____

3. _____

_____

Tools You Can Use!

Tips for Creating an Appeal

1. Begin with a story. This story should relate to the Bible study topic, capture the attention of your audience, connect with them personally, and point them to Jesus! It could be your personal testimony of when you made the decision to be baptized or of when you were afraid of losing your job by keeping the Sabbath but God provided. Or it could be a gripping story of a mother running into a burning house to save her little girl or the dad rushing into the street to save his disobedient son from oncoming traffic.

2. Next, share a Bible verse. Consider using Bible verses that connect with their heart and point them to Jesus. You could use verses such as Jeremiah 29:13; Revelation 3:20; 2 Corinthians 5:17; etc.

3. After reading the Bible text, elaborate to make it personal. Nearly everyone across the United States knows John 3:16—but that doesn't mean it has impacted their lives! Most don't realize how closely this verse relates to them, so be sure to explain the Bible text after reading it, in a way that they can relate to.

4. Finally, ask for a decision! Your decision question should be simple, clear, relate directly to the topic studied, and point them to Christ.

Helpful Questions

In order to know their level of understanding, ask diagnostic questions throughout your Bible study: "Is it clear to you that the seventh day is the Sabbath?" "Do you see from this passage that the rock in Daniel 2 represents Jesus and His everlasting kingdom?" "Do you have any questions?"

Notice we do not ask: "What do you think?" or "Do you like the idea of keeping Sabbath?" We must remember that decisions are never based on our feelings; decisions must be based on the Word of God! Our feelings will follow.

What if they say "no"?

If you have followed the four steps to leading someone to a decision for Christ (captivate, convince, convict, convert) and have asked diagnostic questions, but they still said no to your appeal, what do you do?

Remember to ask this important question: "Is there anything keeping you from making this decision?" They may then list a reason or two. What you next need to determine is if this is the true concern or if they are just making excuses and hiding the real reason. So ask, "If this obstacle were removed, would you then see your way clear to keep the seventh-day Sabbath?" (or whatever decision you are calling them to make). Keep asking variations of this question to get to the core issue before trying to offer a solution.

Include Yourself

First John 1:9 tells us, "If we confess our sins, He is faithful and just to forgive us our sins and to cleanse us from all unrighteousness." Imagine that we are reading this text to David and then we proceed into our appeal like this: "David, you have learned today that if you confess your sins to Jesus—all of the horrible things that you have done—if you'll just give them all to Jesus, He will forgive you. Would you accept this forgiveness?"

How would David feel after an appeal like this? We have just made him feel like an inferior sinner while we stand above him as perfected saints! This is not a positive interaction.

Rather, we must be intentional about including ourselves in the appeal wherever possible. It is easier for our Bible study friends to make decisions when they sense that they are not standing alone. Demonstrate through your appeal that they are standing with both you and Jesus.

Try this revised appeal: "David, today Jesus is promising us that if we confess our sins, He will forgive us. He longs to set us free from the sins of the past and to give us a new life, free from guilt, in Him. Would you join me today in accepting this beautiful forgiveness and a fresh, new start with Jesus?"

Point to Jesus

In every decision, whether it is to keep the Sabbath, to embrace the health message, or to join the remnant church, lift up Jesus Christ! He is and must be the center of every doctrine. Just as you desire to do those things that make your spouse or loved one happy, if someone loves Jesus, he will desire to make decisions that please Him. It will be easier for him to make decisions when he sees how much joy it will bring to the Father's heart.

Words to Live By

Work for the salvation of souls as though you knew by sight that you were in full view of the whole universe of heaven. Every angel in glory is interested in the work being done for the salvation of souls. We are not awake as we should be. All the angelic host are our helpers. "The Lord thy God in the midst of thee, (think of that!) is mighty: he will save: he will rejoice over thee with joy. He will rest in His love: he will joy over thee with singing." O cannot we then work with courage and faith? "In that day it will be said to Jerusalem, Fear thou not: and lo Zion, Let not thine hands be slack." Only have faith. Pray and believe, and ye shall see the salvation of God (Letter 75, 1896).

With an unction of the Holy Spirit upon him, giving him a burden for souls he will not dismiss a congregation without presenting before them Jesus Christ, the sinner's only refuge, making earnest appeals that will reach their hearts. He should feel that he may never meet these hearers again until the great day of God (*Testimonies for the Church*, Vol. 4, p. 315).

God and Jesus, His beloved Son, must be presented before the people in the wealth of the love they have evidenced for man. In order to break down the barriers of prejudice and impenitence, the love of Christ must have a part in every discourse. Make men to know how much Jesus loves them and what evidences He has given them of His love. What love can equal that which God has manifested for man by the death of Christ on the cross. When the heart is filled with the love of Jesus, this can be presented to the people and it will affect hearts (Letter 48, 1886).

Weekly Challenge! This week, actively seek to strengthen the appeals in your Bible studies. Consider:

- Is Christ the center of this study?
- Did I include myself in the appeal, where possible?
- Is it clear? Does it reach the heart?

Never be afraid to ask your Bible study friends to make a decision for Christ. Instead of asking yourself, "What if they say no?" ask yourself, "What if they say yes?" Imagine the joy that will come, both in their lives and in heaven, as they move forward in their relationship with Christ!

When Truth Knocks

A story from Chuck Holtry, AFCOE Director

Anticipation was building on a warm, sunny day in British Columbia, Canada. Church members beamed with excitement as they witnessed their friends and community members walking into the church for the opening night of *Prophecy Speaks Hope.*

Tara and Carrie, two beautiful Filipina sisters with contagious smiles, quickly made themselves at home. This was the first time they had heard many of these incredible truths and they just couldn't get enough! Or so it seemed ...

Though smiling still, the struggle of their hearts was revealed in their eyes. "How will these truths affect our lives?" they silently wondered. Their inner struggle came to a climax as they learned the truth about death, hell, and the millennium. Overwhelmed with confusion and frustration, they cried out to God.

The very next morning, I began to prepare for that day's seminar visitations. As I reviewed the list of names to visit, their names stood out in my mind. There was no doubt God wanted me to visit them that very day! But this task was easier said than done. Upon arriving at their apartment building, it was discovered that they had never actually given us their apartment number. Wandering up to the third floor, I began walking door to door—searching for any indication that this was the home of Tara and Carrie. Out of the corner of my eye, a Christian saying pasted on the front door caught my attention. I quickly knocked. To my surprise and theirs, I had indeed been led to the right door!

"What are you doing here?!" they inquired with surprise written across their faces. After sharing my desire to get to know them better and answer any questions they might have, Tara quickly replied, "You just have no idea! Last night we decided that if someone doesn't come and explain these Bible topics to us, we are done with the seminar!"

Recognizing that this was clearly an answer to their prayers, we sat down and began to study the Bible together, answering all of the questions that had accumulated throughout the prophecy seminar. Peace flooded their souls as their questions were finally answered by the Word of God.

Just two weeks later, on a beautiful spring day, two excited, loving sisters walked into the watery grave of baptism and were raised to a new life! Their joy could not be contained as they went all the way with their God!

Week Eleven
The Gospel Presentation

FOCUS
"If anyone is in Christ, he is a new creation; old things have passed away; behold, all things have become new" (2 Corinthians 5:17).

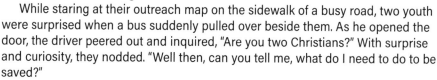

INTRODUCTION

Excitement was building as teams set out for door-to-door outreach on that crisp Sabbath afternoon. Walking and working in pairs, the youth and young adults soon blanketed the entire neighborhood.

While staring at their outreach map on the sidewalk of a busy road, two youth were surprised when a bus suddenly pulled over beside them. As he opened the door, the driver peered out and inquired, "Are you two Christians?" With surprise and curiosity, they nodded. "Well then, can you tell me, what do I need to do to be saved?"

In utter amazement, these two young Christians now had an incredible opportunity to lead this searching bus driver to Jesus!

But how would we respond? Do we even know the answer? How can we encourage others to have a saving relationship with Jesus Christ?

Every Christian should have the assurance of these four great spiritual truths.

1. **His sins are forgiven.** Jesus promised to cleanse us from all unrighteousness (1 John 1:9; Hebrews 8:12).

2. **He has been born again** (John 3:3–5). If you have accepted Christ as your Savior, He makes you into a new creation (2 Corinthians 5:17).

3. **He has received the Holy Spirit into his life** (John 16:7, 13, 14). The same Holy Spirit that brought you into the knowledge of truth will guide you in your new walk with Christ.

4. **He has received eternal life** (Romans 7:24, 25; 1 John 5:13).

This week we will consider how to lead someone into a saving relationship with Christ and give a sound answer to the question, "What must I do to be saved?"

THIS WEEK IN THE SCRIPTURES
Prayerfully read these passages before beginning this week's study.

- Acts 16:25–34
- 2 Timothy 4:6–8
- 1 Peter 1:3–5
- 1 John 5:11–13
- John 6:40, 47
- Acts 3:1–10
- Hebrews 12:1–3

The Assurance of Salvation

Read — Acts 16:25–34

React — What is the prerequisite for salvation? Do we just need to "believe"? (See James 2:17–20.) How was belief exemplified in the jailer's life?

_____

_____

_____

Upon seeing the incredible witness of two joy-filled prisoners on death row being rescued from certain death, the humbled jailer fell down before them and pled, "What must I do to be saved?"

The gentle reply came, "Believe on the Lord Jesus Christ, and you will be saved, you and your household" (Acts 16:31). This newfound belief filled him with joy and led him to action. That very night, he and his entire household followed in the footsteps of Christ and were baptized.

So it should be in our lives. True belief leads to action as we allow God to work through us.

Read — 2 Timothy 4:6–8; 1 Peter 1:3–5; 1 John 5:11–13; John 6:40, 47

React — What do these verses teach us about the assurance of salvation? Did the apostles have this assurance?

_____

_____

_____

When we look at ourselves, we recognize our sinfulness and unworthiness. We may be tempted to question whether we could ever be saved. But when we look to Jesus, in awe and in love, we exclaim, "How could I _not_ be saved?"

Jesus gave everything, all of Himself, so that we could live together with Him for eternity. He longs to bestow the free gift of salvation upon us far more than we even long to have it!

As your conscience has been quickened by the Holy Spirit, you have seen something of the evil of sin, of its power, its guilt, its woe; and you look upon it with abhorrence. You feel that sin has separated you from God, that you are in bondage to the power of evil. The more you struggle to escape, the more you realize your helplessness. Your motives are impure; your heart is unclean. You see that your life has been filled with selfishness and sin.

You long to be forgiven, to be cleansed, to be set free. Harmony with God, likeness to Him—what can you do to obtain it?

It is peace that you need—Heaven's forgiveness and peace and love in the soul. Money cannot buy it, intellect cannot procure it, wisdom cannot attain to it; you can never hope, by your own efforts, to secure it. But God offers it to you as a gift, "without money and without price." Isaiah 55:1. It is yours if you will but reach out your hand and grasp it. The Lord says, 'Though your sins be as scarlet, they shall be as white as snow; though they be red like crimson, they shall be as wool." Isaiah 1:18. "A new heart also will I give you, and a new spirit will I put within you." Ezekiel 36:26. (*Steps to Christ*, p. 49).

Discuss — What other Bible verses might you share with someone questioning whether or not he will be saved or can be saved?

_____

_____

_____

Faith vs. Feeling

Read — Acts 3:1–10 and Mark 2:1–12

React — Upon receiving healing and a glimpse of the character of Christ, how did these men respond? Did others notice the change in their lives?

_____

_____

_____

An apathetic beggar, desiring just a few more coins for his daily sustenance, received a gift greater than he could even imagine! Far more than a healing of his physical ailments, this lonely man received healing of soul as he learned the good news! This indescribable gift could not be contained. To the amazement of the bustling crowd around him, this once-crippled man was "walking, leaping, and praising God"! (Acts 3:8).

So also today, when we experience the joy of salvation, our excitement can't possibly be contained! People all around us will notice and say things like, "There is something different about this person!" That's why, without a doubt, everyone who has a relationship with Christ can lead someone else to Him.

Read — Romans 1:17; Matthew 4:4; Acts 17:10, 11

React — By what must God's children live? Is it ever safe to trust our feelings?

_____

_____

_____

The just do not live by their feelings, they do not live by their emotions, and they do not live by what they can see. The just live by faith. We are pointedly reminded, "Do not wait to _feel_ that you are made whole, but say, 'I believe it; it _is_ so, not because I feel it, but because God has promised'" (_Steps to Christ_, p. 51, emphasis added).

Often, new believers expect that when they accept Christ as their Savior, life will be easier. They feel they will never again be tempted to sin; that they will never make another mistake. And then, when they do, they fall into a pit of despair, wondering if they can ever be good enough to be a Christian.

It is our responsibility and privilege to help new believers understand a powerful principle in Matthew chapters 3 and 4. When Jesus was baptized, He heard the comforting voice of His Father and saw the Spirit descending as a dove upon Him. He experienced perfect peace, joy, and closeness with the Father that day. Yet this perfect moment was immediately challenged as Jesus was led into the wilderness, fasting to the brink of starvation, and being harshly tempted during His weakest moment.

How did Jesus overcome? He believed in every word that proceeded from the mouth of God! In response to each temptation, He claimed Scripture and verbally repeated it. Jesus did not live by His feelings; He did not overcome by His emotion. In His weakest moments—and in His strongest moments—He overcame by the Word of God.

We too must learn to base our relationship with Christ and our assurance of salvation not on our feelings but on the promise of God's Word. He delights to have His children claim His promises as their own! We too are called to live by faith.

Discuss — What three passages would you share with your study friends to encourage them to walk by faith, trusting in God's Word, and not on their feelings? Consider Hebrews 12:1-3, among others.

1. _____

_____

2. _____

_____

3. _____

_____

Is Now the Time?

Read — Acts 10:24–33, 47, 48; 16:27–33; 8:29–38

React — How do we know when it is the right time to share the gospel? What readiness indicators did the individuals in these Bible passages demonstrate?

_____

_____

_____

In each of these instances, the individual was open to how he could receive salvation. The Holy Spirit was already working in their lives, they were listening to His voice, and they were open to truth.

How do we know when it's the right time to share the gospel with our study friends? While there are exceptions to the rule, you should first gain the confidence of the person before presenting the gospel. Remember, Jesus first won the confidence of the people by meeting their *felt needs.* He then probed their inner heart and mind to fulfill their spiritual need.

Follow the voice of the Holy Spirit as you determine the right time to share the gospel. The following questions are good indicators that a person is ready and open to receive Christ. Remember, pray and then watch for the right indicators!

- "How do you pray?"
- "How do I accept Jesus?"
- "Does Jesus really forgive all sins?"
- "What does it really mean to be a Christian?"
- "I've done too much for God to forgive me."
- "I used to know Jesus, but I haven't really prayed in years."
- "I want to know God, but will He really accept me?"

Read — John 12:35, 36

React — When we learn new light, what does Jesus call us to do? According to this passage, what is the risk if we do not follow the light we have been given?

_____

_____

_____

Ellen White warned, "When persons who are under conviction are not brought to make a decision at the earliest period possible, there is danger that the conviction will gradually wear away" (*Evangelism*, p. 298). If your study friends are revealing a spiritual interest, don't delay in sharing the gospel with them! If we don't directly encourage them to listen to the Holy Spirit, that voice may become softer and eventually leave them without light.

How then do we build a bridge to introduce the gospel? Consider the following example:

"John, you mentioned earlier that you don't think God can forgive you for all of the things you've done in the past. Thank you for trusting me enough to share that with me and for being so honest. I'm not going to ask you to tell me what those things are, but could you tell me why you feel that God can't forgive you for them?"

Listen to what John is saying! He will tell you valuable information that you will need to reach his heart.

"John, I know that this feeling of guilt you're experiencing can be overwhelming. I myself have felt it! It is a sobering thought to know that our sins have offended a holy God and that we stand in judgment. Do you know why you feel this way?"

Listen.

"This guilt you feel is a wonderful thing, John, as strange as that sounds. Do you know why? It is because God is dealing with your heart. He is convicting you of sin, and He wants to cleanse you. Do you want to be clean, John? Do you want to make things right with God?"

Listen to his answer.

"God has a special plan by which He can make us clean from sin and to make us right with Him no matter what we have done in the past. He can take away the guilt that we feel and replace it with love, peace, and joy. Not only can He forgive us and cleanse us now, but He can give us strength to overcome in the future. Would you like to know about that plan, John?"

Listen to his response and then proceed with the gospel presentation. Make sure he has his Bible and reads the texts aloud.

Discuss — In your small group, discuss other scenarios you might encounter (e.g., "What does it mean to be a Christian?") and how you can bridge from their question into the gospel presentation.

_____

_____

The Gospel Presentation

Now you are ready to share the gospel presentation with your Bible study friends! How?

Consider using the following passages. Go through this study verse by verse, having them look up and read the verses aloud, if possible. Remember to give a brief explanation after reading each verse; help them to see how these passages are personal to them today! Remember to include personal testimonies, illustrations, and a closing decision question.

1. **No person is exempt — Romans 3:23**

   We may think, "I'm a good person. I've never done anything that bad." But the truth is that we all have sinned. This disease of sin is epidemic worldwide. The Bible teaches that every man and woman on the planet is under the death sentence, because everyone has sinned.

2. **Offend in one point and you're guilty of all — James 2:10**

   It is easy to think that because we have not committed adultery or murdered someone, we really aren't bad sinners. But Jesus brought the Ten Commandments to a deeper level when He said that to even lust for someone is to commit adultery (see Matthew 5:27, 28). As we consider the spiritual application of the law and recognize that to break one of the commandments is to break them all, we can't help but feel our need of grace.

3. **We deserve death — Romans 6:23**

   As a result of our actions of disobedience to God, we have placed ourselves under a sentence of death.

4. **But God calls out to us anyway — Isaiah 59:2, 20, 21**

   Sin separates us from God. But just as in Eden, God keeps calling us back to a relationship with Him. God loves us and does not want us to die. Yet what could God do? He couldn't set aside His law, nor could He ignore sin. To do this would have meant a universe full of chaos. An alternate would be to provide a replacement—someone to die in our place.

5. **He has shown powerful evidence of His love — Romans 5:8**

   God expressed His love for us on Calvary. Jesus Christ was the only person in the universe who could take care of the sin problem.

6. **Jesus is the only way — John 14:6**

   Jesus is the way to salvation. Being a Christian is a little like being married. Traditionally, when a woman marries a man, she takes his last name. When we "marry" Christ through a personal relationship with Him, we take His name by calling ourselves "Christians." Maintaining a good relationship with Jesus is a little like maintaining a good relationship in a marriage: both take consistent communication and faithfulness. The wonderful news about Jesus is the fact that He is always there to communicate to us through the Holy Spirit and He will never leave us.

7. We can be a part of the solution — Ephesians 2:8, 9

We don't have to die. Jesus has given us the choice of life or death. Those who choose life know that they cannot save themselves. Grace is something that we do not deserve but must receive by faith through Jesus, our Savior and Substitute.

8. We can experience freedom — 1 John 1:9

When we confess and repent of our sins, Jesus promises to forgive us freely and to give us power to overcome! There is no sin too great for His love, no temptation too great for His strength. We can experience this fresh start with Him today.

9. We have an invitation to receive His gift — Revelation 3:20

Jesus has been waiting to enter our lives. I can't help but feel that you would like to invite Jesus into your life. (If you have laid a good foundation, the response will be positive). Is that something that you would like to do now? (If he says no, make an appeal. If he says yes, ask if he would like to pray or just repeat a prayer after you.)

10. We have provisions for growth — 2 Corinthians 5:17

Before you leave your study interests, make sure you give them detailed instructions on how to have personal devotional time with God every morning. Prayer and Bible study are the two most important things a new convert can do to strengthen his walk with God. The Gospel of John and the book *Steps to Christ* are a great place to start.

Discuss — Practice giving this Bible study to other members of your class. Remember to make it personal and Christ-centered. Write down two illustrations and one personal testimony that you will include in this gospel presentation.

1. _____

_____

2. _____

_____

3. _____

_____

Tools You Can Use!

Have people ever told you that "just being a good person" is all that's necessary for salvation? They place their salvation experience on their own merit and don't understand the vital points of receiving Christ as their Savior. It's important that every seeker understands the real stakes.

Consider prayerfully asking one of the following three questions to help your study friend grasp the deeper meaning of salvation.

1. How does one become a Christian?

"Mary, I'm so thankful for our studies. I want you to know how much you have helped me as we have shared together from God's Word. You mentioned to me that you have accepted Jesus in your heart. I think that is so awesome, and I believe that you love Him deeply. Mary, could you tell me, according to your understanding of the Bible, how does a person become a Christian?" Note that we do not say anything that would call into question her stated relationship with Christ or criticize her church for not teaching the full gospel!

We want to gently carry a person to a higher level in his relationship with Jesus, not seem like we are telling him that his relationship is not good enough—or that he doesn't have one at all. Always remember that *how* you say it is as important as *what* you say!

It is likely that your study friend will reply, "One becomes a Christian when he believes that Jesus died on the cross for his sins and he asks Him to come into his heart." This is the most common answer. Often confession and repentance, a new life in Christ with a changed heart, victory over sin, a new relationship with Christ, and obedience to God's commandments as a fruit of salvation are left out.

So next ask, "Mary, will you look up a text with me? Let's look up James 2:19. Would you mind reading that text?" Let her read, then say, "We see that even the devil himself believes that Jesus is the Son of God and the Savior of the world. He has even stood by the throne of God! So, Mary, will the devil be in heaven? Do you think that there might be a little more to salvation than 'just believe?' Would you like to see together what the Bible says?" Then lead her through the gospel presentation with an emphasis on confession of sin, repentance, living a new life in Christ by His transforming power, as well as the other portions.

2. If an angel stopped you just outside the pearly gates and asked you why you should be allowed to enter heaven, how would you reply?

The answer to this question almost always reveals if a person truly understands the gospel and righteousness by faith. It will help you evaluate which points in the gospel presentation to emphasize. Remember, you may have to shift the points of emphasis depending on what a person does or doesn't understand.

You also may need to use different illustrations to meet different felt needs. A deeper or simpler explanation may be needed depending on the person's ability to comprehend spiritual things. Again, look for indicators and listen to the Holy Spirit to know which direction to go. If the person seems bored, he may need deeper illustrations. If he is struggling or having a hard time answering the questions, you probably need to simplify things. Different people will respond in different ways. But remember that you don't have to go into every detail with every person. Most people will require only the simple, basic principles of salvation to understand. This is not to be confused with "watering it down." Simple, sound instruction with strong principles is many times more powerful than the deepest Bible study and can be easily accomplished without compromise. That is what makes the gospel so beautiful! It will take experience and practice to get used to it, but the goal is not to be locked into a "script." We need to eventually be flexible and able to read, adapt, and respond to spiritual signals.

3. If we can get to heaven by just being a good person, why, then, did Jesus have to die?
When a person thinks that he can get into heaven just by being a good person, this question points him right back to Christ. There is no real answer except that, "I am really not a good person, but a sinner." It reveals to him that we can't get into heaven by our own merits—only by Christ's.

Once he has realized that he isn't the "good" person he thought he was, you can then lead him in the gospel presentation.

Consider saying, "Mary, it's obvious that there is nothing we can do to get into heaven ourselves. That may seem discouraging, but there is still good news! Would you like to hear God's wonderful plan that will give us assurance that we can be in heaven?"

Words to Live By

"Verily, verily, I say unto you, He that believeth on Me hath everlasting life." Through the beloved John, who listened to these words, the Holy Spirit declared to the churches, "This is the record, that God hath given to us eternal life, and this life is in His Son. He that hath the Son hath life." 1 John 5:11, 12. And Jesus said, "I will raise him up at the last day." Christ became one flesh with us, in order that we might become one spirit with Him. It is by virtue of this union that we are to come forth from the grave,—not merely as a manifestation of the power of Christ, but because, through faith, His life has become ours. Those who see Christ in His true character, and receive Him into the heart, have everlasting life. It is through the Spirit that Christ dwells in us; and the Spirit of God, received into the heart by faith, is the beginning of the life eternal (*The Desire of Ages*, p. 388).

If [Christ] be something He must be everything (C. H. Spurgeon).

I cannot neglect the great salvation that has been brought to me at such an infinite cost to my heavenly Father, who "so loved the world that he gave his only begotten Son, that whosoever believeth in him should not perish, but have everlasting life." I will not dishonor my Redeemer to lightly esteem His sufferings, His trials, His condescension, His sacrifice, His death, because He so loves us, He would Himself become our sin-bearer. Oh, what love, what inexpressible love! He became a man of sorrows, acquainted with grief. He died on the cross [as if He were] a transgressor, that man might be justified through His merits (*Lift Him Up,* p. 215).

Weekly Challenge! Write or chain reference the following passages in your Bible. Pray for a divine appointment and always be prepared to lead others into a personal walk with Jesus!

- Romans 3:23 — All have sinned.
- James 2:10 — Offend in one point, guilty of all.
- Romans 6:23 — Wages of sin is death.
- Isaiah 59:2 — Sin separates us from God.
- Romans 5:8 — While we were yet sinners, Christ died for us.
- John 14:6 — Jesus is the Way, the Truth, the Life.
- Ephesians 2:8, 9 — By grace we are saved through faith.
- 1 John 1:9 — If we confess, He will forgive.
- Revelation 3:20 — Will you open your heart to God today?
- 2 Corinthians 5:17 — We will experience that new life.

A Little Girl's Cry

"Could this really be true?" Tammey cried out to God, pleading for an answer. Regardless of how hard she fought against it, the conviction would not leave. Could she really have been deceived all these years?

Raised in a spiritually conflicted home, Tammey had longed for stability and the answers to her deepest questions. With an atheist father and a Catholic mother, spiritual dissension could be expected. But when a local church began inviting kids to their church, young Tammey had jumped at the opportunity!

This decision made a lasting impact on her life. It was here that she first learned the gospel story and met Jesus as her personal Savior. Several of the churchwomen had adopted her as a spiritual daughter and gave her the gift of her dreams—her very own Bible.

But one day, quite unexpectedly, Tammey's mom had come to a church member's home, picked up Tammey, and never allowed her to return. Heartbroken, Tammey soon began to lose her grasp on God. She found herself in a painful whirlwind of clubbing and drinking, attempting to escape the pain of her childhood. She soon met a man on an equally destructive path. Skinny as a beanpole with huge hair and bright blue eyes, David was hard to miss. Two free spirits united their lives in the search for meaning.

However, the empty naggings of her heart could not be silenced. After receiving an invitation from a friend, Tammey began to attend church again. It wasn't long before the moving descriptions she heard of the death and resurrection of Christ brought Tammey to heartfelt tears, and she once again accepted Jesus as her Savior. Little did she know that her spiritual journey had truly just begun.

While preparing to give a sermon on the book of Revelation, a topic she knew little about, she aimlessly flipped her television on to watch religious programming. She later learned that the speaker was an Adventist evangelist. And what he was saying absolutely amazed her! She had never heard the book of Revelation presented so clearly. She was absolutely convinced this was from God. Tammey soaked up every message and took notes furiously. "Could this really be true?" Tammey wondered.

One day, she heard a loud knock at her door. A middle-aged couple with smiling faces stood on the other side. When Tammey heard that they, Sean and Brenda, were representatives from Amazing Facts, a ministry she was now quite familiar with, she squealed in delight and quickly invited them inside. She later learned that they had come to her home several times and were about to give up, but conviction wouldn't allow them to. This new friendship soon led to Bible studies and an invitation to attend a local prophecy seminar.

One night, after a particularly deep topic, Tammey left the seminar angry. She was battling internally whether or not to accept these truths, finally deciding to never come back. But the team did not give up on her! They continued to pray fervently.

The next night, joy and surprise lit up their faces as Tammey returned to the seminar! She had prayed earnestly for God's guidance, felt at peace that this was indeed His truth, and she planned to follow it with all of her heart.

It wasn't long before Tammey was a member of that local church, but she wasn't about to settle down into a pew! Tammey began to witness to her family, friends, and co-workers of the beautiful things she had learned. Soon she herself was attending the Amazing Facts Center of Evangelism (AFCOE) and knocking on doors too!

As Tammey continues to seek after God, He has never ceased to amaze her. From working as a Bible worker, to teaching as an instructor at AFCOE, to serving as a missionary in Mexico, God has continued to lead and bless the ministry He has given her.

Though many years had passed, God never forgot about the little girl seeking Him who has now found her answer to life's deepest questions.

Week Twelve
Nurturing New Believers

FOCUS

"Shepherd the flock of God which is among you, serving as overseers, not by compulsion but willingly, not for dishonest gain but eagerly; nor as being lords over those entrusted to you, but being examples to the flock" (1 Peter 5:2, 3).

INTRODUCTION

The church should be concerned about proclaiming the gospel; but it should be equally concerned about establishing new believers in the truth and ensuring they are continually growing in their relationship with Jesus.

Conversion, like sanctification, is the work of a lifetime. The baptistery is not the last step of the Christian's experience, but one of the first. It is essential that the church maintain a meaningful discipleship program in which all of the members—new and long-time—are encouraged and strengthened in the Christian walk.

In this lesson, we will discuss ways your church can disciple new believers after an evangelistic series.

Follow-up is equally important as the pre-work and reaping meetings! The true purpose of follow-up is much broader than just keeping new members in the church. It involves fulfilling the great commission to "go therefore and make disciples" (Matthew 28:19, 20).

A disciple does more than assent to the correctness of truth. A disciple is a productive, useful member advancing the cause of God through his or her life.

THIS WEEK IN THE SCRIPTURES

Prayerfully read these passages before beginning this week's study.

- Luke 19:1–10
- Acts 9:1–19
- Hebrews 12:1, 2
- 1 Corinthians 12

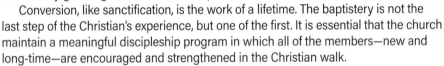

Our First Calling

Read — Mark 3:13, 14

React — What is the first calling that every Christian receives? Why must we be "with Him" before being sent out for ministry?

_____

_____

_____

Just as a plant cannot bear fruit unless it has a strong root system, neither can we expect a harvest of souls—or even bear spiritual fruit ourselves—unless we are deeply rooted in Jesus.

The most powerful Christians are the ones who, when asked to share their testimony, can share what Christ has been doing in their lives that very week or even that very day! Each member must have a living, vibrant relationship with Christ, rooted and grounded in the spirit of divine love, before we are able to share this joyful experience with others.

Read — Luke 19:1-10

React — How did Jesus interact with Zacchaeus, a new believer? What impact did His personal contact have on Zacchaeus' life?

_____

_____

_____

Jesus knew His time on earth was short. There were thousands who needed to hear the good news, yet Christ had less than four years of public ministry available. If we had been His advisors, how quickly we may have suggested: "Jesus, preach only to the multitudes. Don't waste your time on the one-person audience! We can arrange a large rally worthy of Your time."

But this was not Christ's approach; instead, most of His ministry time was spent with small groups or one-on-one interactions! Jesus invested a significant portion of His limited time into twelve quarreling men; He went out of His way to commune with a Samaritan woman of ill repute; He could be found late at night in a garden speaking alone to Nicodemus, a religious leader who was too ashamed to meet Him during the day; and, of course, we find Him brushing away from a large crowd in order to acknowledge one woman who had grasped His robe in faith.

Though some may have seen Jesus' behavior as a waste of time, Jesus recognized that the only way the gospel could truly go to the ends of the earth was through one-on-one discipleship! This concept remains true today.

Discuss — In what other ways did Jesus emphasize the importance of personal discipleship? How have spiritual mentors made an impact on your life?

_____

_____

_____

An Irreplaceable Role

Read — Acts 9:1–19

React — Why did Jesus send Ananias to meet Saul? Couldn't Christ have performed the miracle from heaven since He was the cause of Saul's blindness to begin with? How does Ananias' role compare to ours in ministering to new believers?

_____

_____

_____

How quickly we may have questioned God's call. "You want me to meet *whom*? The man who has been torturing and killing my Christian friends? Lord, don't you know this could be a trick?" Yet Ananias answered the call.

Yes—Jesus could have healed Saul; He could have provided Saul with all of the discipleship he needed, seeing that He had already communicated with him directly from heaven! Yet this was not Christ's chosen method.

Acts of the Apostles, page 122, puts it this way:

When, in the midst of his blind error and prejudice, Saul was given a revelation of the Christ whom he was persecuting, he was placed in direct communication with the church, which is the light of the world. In this case Ananias represents Christ, and also represents Christ's ministers upon the earth, who are appointed to act in His stead. In Christ's stead Ananias touches the eyes of Saul, that they may receive sight. In Christ's stead he places his hands upon him, and, as he prays in Christ's name, Saul receives the Holy Ghost. All is done in the name and by the authority of Christ. Christ is the fountain; the church is the channel of communication.

Read — 1 Peter 5:2–4; 2 Timothy 2:23–25

React — What does it mean to "shepherd the flock"? How did Jesus demonstrate these attributes in His interactions with Peter?

_____

_____

_____

Discuss — "Many have an idea that they are responsible to Christ alone for their light and experience, independent of His recognized followers on earth. Jesus ... has all power, both in heaven and on earth; but He respects the means that He has ordained for the enlightenment and salvation of men;

He directs sinners to the church, which He has made a channel of light to the world" (*The Acts of the Apostles*, p. 122).

What are three ways your local church can be more effective at welcoming and incorporating new believers into the fold?

1. _____

_____

2. _____

_____

3. _____

_____

The Family of Christ

Read — Even an amateur gardener knows that soil must be prepared before seed is planted. Nutrients must then be provided in varying degrees based on the type of plant being grown. Growth should be encouraged by training the vines and through occasional pruning. And last, but certainly not least, the plant must also be protected from the elements and from those pesky insects!

React — How do these lessons from a garden apply to the church? How can we, in a practical manner, 1) prepare the soil of the church for new believers; 2) provide adequate nutrients for these spiritual babes; 3) encourage growth through mentorship; 4) and protect new believers from the attacks of Satan, both from within and without?

_____

_____

_____

Discipleship does not end at the conclusion of the baptismal service; rather, it has just begun! E. G. White records,

> After individuals have been converted to the truth, they need to be looked after. The zeal of many ministers seems to fail as soon as a measure of success attends their efforts. They do not realize that these newly converted ones need nursing,—watchful attention, help, and encouragement. These should not be left alone, a prey of Satan's most powerful temptations; they need to be educated in regard to their duties, to be kindly dealt with, to be led along, and to be visited and prayed with (*Gospel Workers,* p. 92).

Read — Matthew 19:27–29; Mark 10:28–30

React — What is promised to new believers who have left all for Christ? How can the local church family be a partial fulfillment of this prophecy?

_____

_____

_____

When a newborn baby is brought home from the hospital, the parents recognize that their work is not complete; rather, it has truly just begun! There will be many diapers to change, cries to be soothed, and, eventually, scraped knees to be bandaged. This is an expected part of human growth and development.

The same is true with new believers. Now more than ever, new believers, many of whom have left their own biological family behind for the sake of the gospel, need to feel embraced by a church family! As they grow in their experience with Christ, scraped knees are to be expected! Just as a parent gingerly nurtures his child and holds his hand as he takes his first wobbly steps, we as a church family must be intentional about nurturing these spiritual babes!

Discuss — It is easy for new believers to become discouraged, especially if their biological family is not supportive of their new relationship with Christ. How can we encourage them during this time? (See Hebrews 12:1, 2.)

_____

_____

_____

Spiritual Gifts

Read — 1 Corinthians 12:1, 4-11

React — Why are spiritual gifts given to God's people? Who decides what spiritual gift(s) we receive?

_____

_____

_____

The Holy Spirit, not church members, determines which spiritual gifts are bestowed upon each individual. These gifts are not to be hoarded or used for our own benefit; rather, they are given for the "profit of all" (1 Corinthians 12:7). But how few new believers (or even seasoned believers) understand their own spiritual gifts and the great importance of utilizing them for the building up of the kingdom of God! As the apostle Paul said, these gifts should be used "till we all come to the unity of the faith and of the knowledge of the Son of God, to a perfect man, to the measure of the stature of the fullness of Christ." (See also Ephesians 4:1-6, 11-16.)

The liberality of the sower illustrates this principle:

The sower multiplies his seed by casting it away. So it is with those who are faithful in distributing God's gifts. By imparting they increase their blessings. God has promised them a sufficiency that they may continue to give. "Give, and it shall be given unto you; good measure, pressed down, and shaken together, and running over, shall men give into your bosom." Luke 6:38. (*Christ's Object Lessons*, p. 85).

Our gifts are received and strengthened in accordance with how freely we give them away in the service of others!

Read — 1 Corinthians 12:12-30

React — Is the role of one person more important than that of another? How can we encourage new believers to recognize the importance of their gifts and to utilize them in ministry?

_____

_____

_____

Jeremiah said, "His word was in my heart like a burning fire shut up in my bones; I was weary of holding it back, and I could not" (Jeremiah 20:9). How often this fire in the bones is witnessed in new believers! (And, we hope, in long-time believers too!) They seemingly come out of the baptismal water on fire! Now is the time to direct this passion and joy into service for God, lest it be quenched.

Discuss — Why is it so important to provide opportunities for new believers to quickly become involved in the church body? How does our faith strengthen when we utilize our spiritual gifts?

_____

_____

_____

Tools You Can Use!

What are some things that a spiritual mentor should do?

1. Get to know new members and genuinely befriend them.

2. Greet new members at every church service and program—and invite them to stay for fellowship dinner at the church or at your home.

3. Implement a spiritual guardianship plan with pastors and elders.

4. Look for ways to involve new members in church programs and activities.

5. Introduce new members to established members of the church.

6. Speak positively of the church, pastor, conference, etc.

7. Encourage new believers in the faith.

Apply! — Here are five sample activities you can utilize to disciple new believers:

1. Make regular phone calls or schedule personal visits.

2. Invite new members home for Sabbath dinner once a month. Include other members who may have things in common with the new members. This will help the new member become acquainted with more people in the church.

3. During the week, invite the new member to meet you for lunch at a local restaurant.

4. Do social activities together. If you are planning a day of recreation, include your new members. Train yourself to think in terms of including new members in all of these activities!

5. Sit with your new member friends in church, at fellowship meals, and at other church functions.

   A simple yet vital part of being a spiritual mentor is to introduce new members to other church members.

   For instance, you can simply say to the new member, "I want you to meet

   _____."

   Say to the established member, "John, have you met [the new member]?"

   Turning to the new member, say something interesting, such as, "John runs a contracting company in town," to get the conversation going.

Words to Live By

It is not in God's purpose that the church shall be sustained by life drawn from the minister. They are to have root in themselves. The gospel news, the message of warnings, the third angel's message, is to be voiced by church members (*Evangelism*, p. 343).

After the first efforts have been made in a place by giving a course of lectures, there is really greater necessity for a second course than for the first. The truth is new and startling, and the people need to have the same presented the second time, to get the points distinct and the ideas fixed in the mind (*Evangelism*, p. 334).

Learn the art of loving men to Christ! We are drawn towards those who love us and when the most callous feel "that man loves us," they are drawn to you at once—and as you are nearer to the Savior than they are—you are drawing them in the right direction. You cannot look after God's people and properly care for them in all their sins, temptations, trials and difficulties, unless you love them (Sermon by C. H. Spurgeon, April 13, 1877).

Weekly Challenge! This week, invite a new believer and his or her family to your house for a meal. Be intentional about also including a second church family who has similar interests as the new believer! Find out what the new believer's spiritual gifts are and look for ways to utilize these strengths in the church, helping the new believer become involved in a local church ministry.

The Pardoned Prostitute, Part One

The fear in her eyes could not be disguised. She scanned the room anxiously, looking for the closest exit in case she was forced to make her escape. With one last glance toward the speaker, she eased into her seat in the back of the church.

Ruby* was quickly noticed by all the other attendees. With her dyed red hair styled as large as Texas and clothing several sizes too small, blending into the crowd did not seem to be her aim. Even her thick makeup couldn't cover the evidence of the rough life she had endured, nor of the pain expressed in her eyes. Other eyes may have stared at her, but Ruby's eyes were fixed in another direction altogether. She leaned forward in her seat, staring straight ahead, entirely engrossed as she heard Jesus revealed through the book of Revelation.

As soon as the meeting closed that night, Amazing Facts Center of Evangelism students introduced themselves and befriended this once terrified attendee. Upon learning that she did not have a ride home, the offer was quickly made. Little did the driver know that the meager home at the end of a dark street was no typical residence; it was the home of Ruby's pimp.

Ruby was a prostitute, selling sex for drugs.

Insults and threats from her pimp were not enough to dissuade Ruby from this seminar. She continued to faithfully attend and accepted the beautiful new truths she was learning. From the moment the seminar handbill first reached her hands, she knew she had to come. For years she had been terrified about the coming of Christ and Armageddon. "What is the mark of the beast?" "Does the Bible say anything about terrorism?" These were the questions voiced from her lips, but her heart craved answers to even deeper questions still: "Will God forgive me for abandoning my children? After years of prostitution and drug abuse, can I ever be good enough for God?"

These questions continued to nag silently at her heart ...

Continued next week ...

*Name has been changed.

Week Thirteen
Reclaiming Missing Members

FOCUS
"What man of you, having a hundred sheep, if he loses one of them, does not leave the ninety-nine in the wilderness, and go after the one which is lost until he finds it?" (Luke 15:4).

INTRODUCTION

The rumble of excitement filled the courtyard. "I never knew Him!" the shout of the betrayer could be heard as it rang out above the crowd. Suddenly, every voice was hushed, a deathly silence blanketing the courtyard, as all eyes turned toward the man who had once stood as Christ's defender.

Now oblivious to all others, Peter stood motionless as his gaze suddenly caught the pained expression of a Man who had loved him as no other. The tender, loving compassion held in that brief glance cut through him like no weapon ever could. With a groan of agony, he turned in haste and fled as the gentle eyes of Jesus looked on and the painful blows continued to fall upon His torn flesh.

Just a few short days had passed since this tragic scene, yet so much had occurred. Jesus had been crucified and hung upon a wooden cross, but now He had risen as a conqueror from the dead. And yet, in a message given to three women through an angel on that resurrection morning, Jesus inspired hope and acceptance in Peter once again: "Go, tell His disciples—and Peter—that He is going before you into Galilee; there you will see Him" (Mark 16:7).

Though Peter was guilty of the deepest betrayal, Jesus still accepted him with open arms into His inner circle. Jesus still included him among His disciples! We are told ...

In every human being He discerned infinite possibilities. He saw men as they might be, transfigured by His grace—in "the beauty of the LORD our God." Psalm 90:17. Looking upon them with hope, He inspired hope, meeting them with confidence, He inspired trust. Revealing in Himself man's true ideal, He awakened, for its attainment, both desire and faith. In His presence souls despised and fallen realized that they still were men, and they longed to prove themselves worthy of His regard (*Education*, p. 80).

Many Peters live in this world today, individuals who once stood close to Jesus but have since drifted or have torn themselves apart from Him. Jesus does not push them aside; they are not forgotten. Rather, He actively pursues them while seeking to bring them back to the safety and joy of the fold. Are we following in the footsteps of the Good Shepherd? Are we being used by God to bring His wayward children back into a saving relationship with Him?

This week we will learn why former members have left the church and dive into very practical principles for bringing them back. By the grace of God, we will see many—like Peter—transformed into powerful soul winners for Him!

THIS WEEK IN THE SCRIPTURES

Prayerfully read these passages before beginning this week's study.

- Jeremiah 29:11–13
- Matthew 10:5, 6
- Acts 1:8, 9
- Luke 15:3–32
- John 20:24–29

Seeking to Save

Read — Exodus 25:8; Jeremiah 29:11-13; Romans 5:8

React — How did God respond when Adam and Eve rejected Him? Does God ever give up? How would we know if He did?

_____

_____

_____

Though Adam and Eve knowingly chose a piece of fruit over loyalty to Him, Jesus lovingly assured the couple of the promise of His future sacrifice, symbolized through the death of that first precious lamb. Even in the midst of their complaints and idolatry, Jesus instructed the Israelites to make a sanctuary that He might dwell among them. When the sins of His people led them into Babylonian captivity, Jesus nonetheless offered them a beautiful future and a reminder that God was still thinking of them. And though we were entrenched in our sins, Christ died for us.

The whole gospel story has revealed a God of infinite love, One who continues to actively pursue those who have hurt Him most. God never gives up on us! Oh that we would have that same loving passion for others.

Read — Matthew 10:5, 6; Acts 1:8, 9

React — When Jesus sent out His disciples, where did He instruct them to go first? Did He apply this same approach in His own ministry?

_____

_____

_____

The focus of Christ's ministry on earth was in reclaiming the lost sheep of the house of Israel. He began where He was, with those who had some understanding of the truth, and then He went farther and then farther still to Samaria.

Yet how often in our ministry endeavors we begin in the "uttermost parts of the earth" while bypassing the lost sheep right beside us! God is calling us to start where we are.

There's good news: The Holy Spirit is convicting former members of your church to return. These non-attending members are "ripe" for an invitation to come home!

When the storm of persecution really breaks upon us, the true sheep will hear the true Shepherd's voice. Self-denying efforts will be put forth to save the lost, and many who have strayed from the fold will come back to follow the great Shepherd (*Evangelism*, p. 693).

Discuss — How did Jesus minister to "missing members" during His brief but effective years of public ministry? What are three methods that we can apply in our local church?

1. _____

_____

2. _____

_____

3. _____

_____

Bitter or Better Ministry

Read — Luke 15:3–32

React — What three stories are recorded in Luke 15? What three categories of people do these stories represent?

_____

_____

_____

Much like those in the world who have never met Christ, the coin did not recognize its lost condition, nor did it know where to go. The lamb, on the other hand, knew it was lost but it was unable to find its way home, signifying many who are seeking a purpose for their lives but don't know where to go to find the answer. Finally, the story of the prodigal son best represents those who were once close to Christ but have since wandered from Him. They know they are lost and they know where to go, but without the Father's welcoming arms, they might not make that trip home.

Though we would like to compare ourselves to the loving father who warmly welcomes home his filthy son, how often we actually resemble the older brother in that story! We may doubt the sincerity of the missing member upon his return to the fold—"Oh, he's done this before. It won't be long before he's back at his old lifestyle." Or maybe we hold a grudge against him for all of his past decisions.

Ellen White once recorded a similar experience:

Some of the church had no special anxiety to see Brother A return. They cared not enough to unbend from their dignity and pride and make special efforts to help him to the light. They stood back in their dignity and said, "We will not go after him; let him come to us." Viewing the feeling of his brethren toward him as he did, it was impossible for him to do this. Had they regarded the lesson taught by Christ, they would have been willing to yield their dignity and pride, and go after the wandering ones. They would have wept over them, prayed for them, implored them to be faithful to God and the truth, and to abide with the church. But the feeling of many was, "If he wants to go, let him go" (*Testimonies for the Church*, Vol. 2, p. 218).

Discuss — According to this quote, how should we respond to those who have left the faith? How can we overcome the bitterness or disappointments from past interactions with them? What is the Bible's counsel for restoring these relationships?

_____

_____

_____

Ministering to the Doubting Thomas

Read — John 20:24–29

React — After being in the presence of Jesus for more than three years and seeing Him work countless miracles, why did Thomas experience doubt? How did Jesus respond to his doubt?

_____

_____

_____

"Do not be unbelieving, but believing," Jesus encouraged as He offered His scarred hand and side to the doubting disciple. Though his doubt may seem unforgivable to us, Jesus did not condemn Thomas; rather, He gave him encouragement to believe.

Likewise, we need to recognize that believers need frequent encouragement and support, regardless of how long they have been on their spiritual journey. Indeed, a lack of supportive relationships is the number one reason why people leave the church.

Consider — Why do Seventh-day Adventists leave the church?

- A conflict with the pastor or a church member
- Discouragement over personal problems and/or discouragement with themselves over failure to live in harmony with Bible standards
- A growing disinterest in spiritual things because of a neglected personal devotional and prayer life
- The perception that the church is no longer relevant in their life and does not meet their needs
- Deep, personal tragedy, which leads to a questioning of God or frustration at the lack of support offered by the church

Notice that the majority of missing members have not left because of a doctrinal question, but rather because of a poor interpersonal relationship with someone in the church or with Christ.

Discuss — How would you respond if someone tells you he doesn't want to go to church because of all of the hypocrites? Hint: Were the disciples flawless? Did the early church have challenges? How did Christ use and transform them?

_____

_____

_____

One Empty Chair

Read — Luke 15:4

React — How long does the shepherd continue searching? Is one lamb really that significant of a loss, considering he owns ninety-nine others?

_____

_____

_____

How often we are tempted to feel as though we are of little consequence. In a world of seven billion people, how could one person be that important? Yet the sacrifice of Christ reveals the stunning worth of every soul!

Imagine sitting down for an annual holiday dinner with your family—the first reunion since the unexpected death of your younger sister. Your mother smiles as she looks down the long oak table at each person seated there. "It's too bad my daughter died," the mother states with a smile still stretched across her face, "but it really doesn't matter because I have all of you here."

Can you picture such a scene? Impossible! Regardless of how many children she has or how many guests are seated at the table, the heart of the mother is forever pained at the absence of her little girl.

So it is with Christ! Regardless of how many people are seated at the heavenly table, the one empty chair represents a heart-breaking loss to Him. "There will be more joy in heaven over one sinner who repents than over ninety-nine just persons who need no repentance" (Luke 15:7).

Consider — There are three basic steps in reclaiming lost members:

1. Get names and find out why people left.
2. Visit former members and seek to reclaim them, listening to them, and inviting them to events.
3. Nurture these new believers into a renewed commitment to Christ and His church.

How do you locate non-attending members?

1. Church records
2. Referrals from Adventist relatives/friends
3. Church school records
4. In large congregations, many names on the church books may not be recognized by church board members. Probably the simplest way to

discover who these people are is to distribute a list of unfamiliar names to the church members, asking them to fill in any information they have about names on the list.

Tips for Visitation

1. It's a good idea to always visit in pairs. "God never designed that, as a rule, His servants should go out singly to labor" (*Evangelism,* p. 73).

2. Wherever possible, "match up" visiting members with the ones being visited according to similar interests, careers, family backgrounds, etc.

3. Consult closely with your pastor before setting out on your mission.

Discuss — In what other ways can we reconnect with missing members?

_____

_____

_____

Tools You Can Use!

Your heart begins to race. With sweaty palms, you remove your seatbelt yet remain invisibly attached to your seat, staring at the seemingly impenetrable front door standing between you and the missing member. What do you say? How can you build a relationship with this missing member? Where do you start?

First and foremost—pray! Pull over before you are within view of the house and pray for the Holy Spirit's guidance.

When you go to the door, you can say something like this:

"Hi! I'm _____ and this is _____. We're with the _____ Seventh-day Adventist Church. We wanted to come by and get acquainted."

Be friendly and warm but not gushy. If they invite you inside, ask about their job, family, and anything else that may come to your attention. After a few minutes, or when it comes up naturally in conversation, ask:

"You used to attend our church. How long ago was that? Have you ever thought about coming back to our church?"

This could open up a lengthy discussion. Listen attentively, making sure you hear all they have to say. Reassure them that the church family will seek a resolution if needed and wants to see them back again. Before you leave, be sure to invite them to any future church events that might interest them.

Consider — A few DOs:

1. Get to the point of your visit within a few minutes.
2. Listen kindly; listen interestedly; listen calmly.
3. Always close your visit with prayer.
4. Give a brief invitation to come out to the evening seminar meeting or to church the next Sabbath.
5. Leave immediately after prayer.

Close your visit with something like this:

"Well, we must be going. [That statement always relaxes people!] But before we leave, let's just bow our heads for a moment of prayer."

As you are saying this, just bow your head and start praying a short, sincere prayer. In your prayer, you can say things like, "Help us as we grow in our relationship with You." "Forgive us for the hurt we have caused others and help us to experience Your healing power in our lives." And remember this promise:

The redeemed will be sharers in His joy, as they behold, among the blessed, those who have been won to Christ through their prayers, their labors, and their loving sacrifice (*The Great Controversy,* p. 647).

When inviting them to a church event, don't try to squeeze out a promise that they will attend. This will undo the good you have done. Your whole visit should be conducted in a casual, friendly way, endeavoring to leave former members relaxed, with a knowledge that you really love them and care about their return.

Consider — A few DON'Ts:

1. Don't betray their confidence.
2. Don't act shocked.
3. Don't defend anyone.
4. Don't stay long—ten to fifteen minutes is usually long enough.
5. Don't dismiss backsliders as hopeless.
6. Don't argue about church standards. Nurture—don't argue—them back.

Consider — What next? After your initial visit ...

1. Put their names on the church list for social events—but not solicitation events!
2. Stay in touch. From time to time, telephone former members, keeping them informed about interesting church-family news.
3. Use important upcoming events as an excuse for a return visit to invite them. Bring along someone in their age group with similar interests to get acquainted.
4. Help solve personal problems that obstruct church attendance, such as babysitting, transportation, or care-giving. Take a personal interest in their children.
5. If appropriate, occasionally stop by their home with a book, a loaf of bread, or a basket of fruit.
6. Put forth every effort in your power to see that former members are present during a call for surrender or at a special Sabbath morning consecration or baptism service.
7. If the family has financial needs, present them to the appropriate church leaders/department for resolution.

If a first visit goes well but the missing members don't want a follow-up visit, you can give them a copy of a non-threatening book. Be sure to have your phone number written inside in case they want to contact you. Then allow the Holy Spirit to work on them through the printed word.

Words to Live By

Have you, reader, chosen your own way? Have you wandered far from God? Have you sought to feast upon the fruits of transgression, only to find them turn to ashes upon your lips? And now, your substance spent, your life-plans thwarted, and your hopes dead, do you sit alone and desolate? Now that voice which has long been speaking to your heart but to which you would not listen comes to you distinct and clear, "Arise ye, and depart; for this is not your rest; because it is polluted, it shall destroy you, even with a sore destruction." Micah 2:10. Return to your Father's house. He invites you, saying, "Return unto Me; for I have redeemed thee." Isaiah 44:22.

Do not listen to the enemy's suggestion to stay away from Christ until you have made yourself better; until you are good enough to come to God. If you wait until then, you will never come. When Satan points to your filthy garments, repeat the promise of Jesus, "Him that cometh to Me I will in no wise cast out." John 6:37. Tell the enemy that the blood of Jesus Christ cleanses from all sin. Make the prayer of David your own, "Purge me with hyssop, and I shall be clean; wash me, and I shall be whiter than snow." Psalm 51:7.

Arise and go to your Father. He will meet you a great way off. If you take even one step toward Him in repentance, He will hasten to enfold you in His arms of infinite love. His ear is open to the cry of the contrite soul. The very first reaching out of the heart after God is known to Him. Never a prayer is offered, however faltering, never a tear is shed, however secret, never a sincere desire after God is cherished, however feeble, but the Spirit of God goes forth to meet it. Even before the prayer is uttered or the yearning of the heart made known, grace from Christ goes forth to meet the grace that is working upon the human soul (*Christ's Object Lessons,* pp. 205, 206).

Weekly Challenge! Do you have family members or friends who have left their faith in God? Are there missing members in your community? This week, personally visit one or two of these individuals. Seek to restore any lost relationships, listen to objections, involve them in upcoming church activities, and encourage them in their own personal spiritual journey. Depending on their situation, prayerfully consider starting small group or individual Bible studies with them as well!

The Pardoned Prostitute, Part Two

In last week's story, we met Ruby*, a drug-addicted prostitute who began to attend a local prophecy seminar. Though once timid, her fears were melted away by the church's warm reception and the beautiful message of Christ revealed through the book of Revelation ...

Students of the Amazing Facts Center of Evangelism (AFCOE) and church members gathered in a small room, pressing closely together with comforting hands laid across the shoulders of a desperate woman. Although Ruby had moved out of her pimp's house, she was still under his oppressive control. She knew that her very life was in danger. But even that fear was not enough to hold her back from this desperate escape from the deep pit of sin and pain.

Not long into the seminar, Ruby began to experience the joy of victory and healing! Each night she began to proudly update AFCOE students, as a smile lit up her face: "Five days without drugs!" "Clean for seven days!" "No drugs now for ten days!" she gleefully declared. How incredible it was to see her contagious joy as Jesus truly set her free!

But that particular night, following the appeal, Ruby remained fastened to her seat. The struggle in her heart was clear; the great controversy was real. Quietly a church member slipped onto the pew beside her. Ruby looked up with eyes brimmed with tears. As the member put an arm around her shoulders, Ruby melted: "I've just done so much! I'm so dirty. How can I be a Christian?" she cried. Her eyes begged for answers as tears ran freely down her cheeks.

"Ruby, tonight God has a special promise in His Word just for you!" her friend earnestly replied. She quickly turned to 2 Corinthians 5:17 and read, 'If anyone is in Christ, he is a new creation: old things have passed away; behold, all things have become new.' Ruby, when Jesus looks at you, He does not see a former drug addict. He does not see a former prostitute. He sees a virgin! Because we serve a Creator God who makes all things new!"

Ruby sat up in peaceful silence as these words began to sink deep into her heart. She was of value! She was a beautiful, pure woman! Truly Christ had made her new.

The cool autumn air greeted the students Sabbath morning as they filed into church. Anticipation was building. It wasn't long before tears began to flow freely as a beautiful woman with bright red hair stepped into the baptismal tank. Every heart soared with joy as Ruby came out of that cool water a fresh, new woman in Jesus! A woman genuinely transformed by the love of her Savior—her life a living testament to brokenness made beautiful in the hands of our Creator God.

*Name has been changed.

The *NEW* Amazing Facts Bible Study Guides

BRAND NEW!

They have already helped tens of thousands discover the truth of the last-day message—but now our popular set of 27 Bible Study Guides just got even better with fresh, vibrant graphics and updated content! Each encouraging lesson points seekers to new life in the Savior! Easy and fun to use, your interests will gain a clear understanding of Bible doctrines step by step. Excellent for personal study or with a group, these winsome, uplifting lessons can be shared as individual topical studies or as part of an overall church outreach effort. The possibilities are endless and the results are eternal!

Product Code: SG-CSET

Winsome Witnessing

Author Gary Gibbs illuminates useful how-to instruction with inspiring and humorous stories from his witnessing adventures to help you become a better, more effective soul winner for Jesus. Here you will learn simple skills to lead people Christ, insights to revitalize your church, a proven ~ategy to give interesting Bible studies, and much ~ore. This practical manual is sure to energize your ~lationship with God.   **Product Code: BK-WW**

Answers to Difficult Bible Texts

Joe Crews. Get real-world, vital answers to 100 perplexing Bible verses with a quick and handy index. Answers the many apparent contradictions that confound seekers, including about the Sabbath, and many more challenging subjects. No study or witnessing library is complete without it!

Product Code: BK-ANS

Shop and Grow at AFBookstore.com!

The Amazing Facts Bookstore is dedicated to sharing the gospel of Jesus Christ and the three angels' messages of Revelation 14 with the entire world. Our fully stocked bookstore provides trustworthy, effective Bible study resources for the entire family!

At AFBookstore.com, you'll find:

- Bibles and Study Guides for all ages
- Cookbooks and more on healthy living
- Resources for kids and for family life
- Devotionals, documentaries, and music
- Prophecy seminars, witnessing materials, and much more!

AFBookstore.com is the perfect, affordable, user-friendly place for you to order solid, biblical materials as gifts, for witnessing, and for your own Christian growth.